D. G. MAR

North Carolina's

EATERIES

A Traveler's Guide to Local Restaurants, Diners, and Barbecue Joints

THE UNIVERSITY OF NORTH CAROLINA PRESS

Chapel Hill

LIBRARY OF CONGRESS CATALOGING-IN-PUBLICATION DATA
Names: Martin, D. G. (David Grier), 1940– author.
Title: North Carolina's roadside eateries : a traveler's guide to local
    restaurants, diners, and barbecue joints/by D. G. Martin.
Other titles: Southern gateways guide.
Description: Chapel Hill : The University of North Carolina Press, [2016]
    | Series: A Southern gateways guide
Identifiers: LCCN 2016019441 | ISBN 9781469630144 (pbk : alk. paper)
    | ISBN 9781469630151 (ebook)
Subjects: LCSH: Restaurants—North Carolina—Guidebooks.
    | Roads—North Carolina—Guidebooks.
Classification: LCC TX907.3.N8 M37 2016 | DDC 647.95756—dc23
    LC record available at https://lccn.loc.gov/2016019441

For Harriet Wall Martin; our children and their spouses, Grier and Louise Martin and Cotton and May Bryan; and our grandchildren, Sara Louise Martin, Margaret May Bryan, Jacob Grier Bryan, and David Wall Bryan.

Contents

Foreword xiii

Introduction 1

Interstate 26 7

Little Creek Cafe 8

Wagon Wheel 9

Moose Cafe 10

Harry's Grill and Piggy's Ice Cream 12

Ward's Grill 14

Green River Bar-B-Que 15

Caro-Mi Dining Room 16

Interstate 40 19

Clyde's Restaurant 20

Sherrill's Pioneer Restaurant 21

Little Pigs Bar-B-Q 22

Luella's Bar-B-Que 23

12 Bones Smokehouse 25

Louise's Kitchen 26

Countryside BBQ 27

Judge's Riverside 28

Hursey's Bar-B-Q 29

Snack Bar 30

Sunshine's Café 32

Keaton's BBQ 33

Miller's Restaurant 36

Deano's Barbecue 37

The Diner 38

Little Richard's BBQ 40

La Botana Home Made Mexican Food 41

Sweet Potatoes 43

The Plaza Restaurant 45

Prissy Polly's Pig Pickin' BBQ 46

Stamey's Old Fashioned Barbecue 47

Smith Street Diner 49

Allen & Son 50

Margaret's Cantina 52

Backyard BBQ Pit 53

Neomonde Raleigh Café/Market 55

Pam's Farmhouse Restaurant 56

State Farmers Market Restaurant 57

Toot-n-Tell Restaurant 58

Stephenson's Bar-B-Q 60

Meadow Village Restaurant 62

The Country Squire 63

Holland's Shelter Creek Fish Camp 64

Paul's Place Famous Hot Dogs 65

Casey's Buffet 67

Interstates 73 & 74 69　　Blake's Restaurant 71

Dixie III Restaurant 72

America's Roadhouse 73

Johnson's Drive-In 74

Soprano's 76

Snyder Farms Restaurant 77

Hill's Lexington Barbecue 78

Snappy Lunch 79

Interstate 77 81　　John's Family Restaurant 83

Lupie's Café 84

The Open Kitchen 85

Acropolis Cafe & Grille 87

The Soda Shop 89

Isy Bell's Cafe 91

Lancaster's Bar-B-Que 93

Julia's Talley House 94

Carolina Bar-B-Q 95

The Cook Shack 97

The Lantern Restaurant 98

Interstate 85 99　　Mountain View Restaurant 101

Alston Bridges Barbecue 102

Red Bridges Barbecue Lodge 103

Shelby Cafe 104

R. O.'s Bar-B-Cue 105

Kyle Fletcher's Barbeque & Catering 106

Hillbilly's BBQ & Steaks 107

Catfish Cove 108

United House of Prayer for All People 110

Townhouse II 111

Troutman's Bar-B-Q 112

Gary's Bar-B-Cue 114

Porky's Bar-B-Q 115

Wink's King of Barbecue 117

Richard's Bar B-Q 118

College Barbecue 119

Backcountry Barbeque 120

Lexington Barbecue, Lexington 121

Bar-B-Q Center 123

Southern Lunch 124

Tommy's Bar-B-Que 125

Captain Tom's Seafood Restaurant 126

Pioneer Family Restaurant
and Steakhouse 127

Mary B's Southern Kitchen 128

Kepley's Bar-B-Q 129

Jack's Barbecue 131

Hursey's Pig-Pickin' Bar-B-Q 132

Angelo's Family Restaurant 133

Hillsborough BBQ Company 134

Bennett Pointe Grill & Bar 136

Bullock's Bar-B-Cue 137

Saltbox Seafood Joint 139

Bob's Bar-B-Q 141

BBQ Barn 142

Skipper Forsyth's Bar-B-Q 143

Nunnery-Freeman Barbecue 144

Whistle Stop Cafe 145

Interstate 95 *147*

Linda's *149*

Sheff's Seafood Restaurant *150*

Candy Sue's Restaurant *151*

Fuller's Old Fashion Bar-B-Q,
Lumberton *152*

Tarpackers Restaurant *154*

Fuller's Old Fashioned Bar-B-Q,
Fayetteville *155*

Broad Street Deli and Market *156*

Sherry's Bakery *157*

Miss Maude's Cafe *158*

Holt Lake Bar-B-Q & Seafood *159*

White Swan Bar-B-Q & Fried Chicken *160*

The Diner *161*

Wilber's Barbecue *163*

Bill's Barbecue and Chicken
Restaurant *164*

Parker's Barbecue, Wilson *165*

Gardner's Barbecue *167*

Smith's Red and White Restaurant *168*

Ralph's Barbecue *170*

Broadnax Diner *172*

Afterword 173

Acknowledgments 175

Foreword

"All great literature is one of two stories; a man goes on a journey or a stranger comes to town," wrote Russian writer Leo Tolstoy.

This little book may not be great literature, but it can open a way for you to make your own great stories, ones you can experience in your journeys along North Carolina highways when you become the stranger who comes to town to visit a local eatery and local people.

You can find information about more than 100 restaurants on the following pages. Still, this book is not primarily a book about food and certainly not a typical food guide. Rather, it is about community gathering places where food is also served.

If the book is successful, it will only be because it persuades you to do something different at mealtime when you are traveling, to be a journeying stranger and eat where locals come together.

The rewards will be bountiful memories. You will have stories you made for yourself, ones that you will remember long after you have forgotten stories other people wrote.

Introduction

Just where did I learn that local restaurants are where you find real friends and lifelong memories?

Maybe it was my North Mecklenburg High School football teammate Tommy Oehler who got me started when he introduced me to his dad, J. W., and the wonders of the annual Mallard Creek Church barbecue, which the Oehler family still manages every October north of Charlotte. There is no better example of how good barbecue and a host of friendly people make a meal into something memorable.

My whole life, to this day, I'm still on the lookout for places where I can find the Mallard Creek feeling. The places I've found that live up to Mallard Creek, at least in my mind—the restaurants that are about food, friends, and more—are the places you'll find in this book. So when I ask just where did I learn that local restaurants are where you find real friends and lifelong memories, I suppose my answer would be North Carolina is where. I have a lifetime's worth of memories about the food and friendship in this state, and they led me to write this book.

I'll tell you how Charlotte's Open Kitchen gave my Davidson College basketball teammates refuge and fellowship after a disappointing loss on New Year's Eve. Those memories of their robust red sauce and pasta, classic pizzas, and that open doorway to the bustling kitchen have always make me want to find similar eateries in other parts of our state.

1

When Lefty Driesell became our coach, he usually took the team out for supper after the games. We had simple meals at the kinds of local eateries I came to love, like the ones in this book. But after we began my senior season with six straight losses, out of desperation he promised to give us a steak dinner after every game we won. Right then, we started winning and, more importantly, enjoying the steaks. But after our twelfth straight win, Lefty confessed that he had spent the whole of his travel budget on our steak dinners. The steaks would have to stop. Immediately, we lost our next game to underdog VMI, with me taking and missing a last shot that would have tied the game. No steak, no streak.

When I was in the army, stationed at Fort Bragg, the Haymont Grill in Fayetteville became a second home. Great juicy fried chicken, meat loaf with two vegetables, rolls, and tea filled me up for under a dollar. Owner Pete Skenteris befriended me and helped me fit in with the locals. He still does, but he now charges more than a dollar for the meat-and-two-vegetables plate. It's still delicious and always fresh.

In Charlotte practicing law, my friends and I shunned the fancy places. We favored a modest diner on South Tryon called Jake's. Jake's is long gone, but my former law partners still remember the "Number 5 hamburger plate" and the over-the-top "One on a Plate," which was a slice of just-made apple pie and a scoop of ice cream. The owner took care of us like important people even though we were not. But when I ran for Congress in 1984 and he saw one of our TV ads, he stopped me on the street to say, "Great ad, D. G. You look a lot better on TV than you do in person."

Law practice put me on the road regularly, and I found restaurant after restaurant that served homey, delicious food. Once, on the way from Charlotte to Greensboro, a client made me stop at his favorite barbecue place, Lexington #1. Wayne Monk and his friendly crew instantly made me feel at home. And the chopped plate with slaw and baked beans, plus the hot, crisp hushpuppies, suited me better than anything I had ever eaten. Thank goodness it is still there.

That same client told me about the delicious slaw at R. O.'s Bar-B-Cue in Gastonia. So good, he said, that he was going to open a restaurant that sold slaw burgers made with R. O.'s slaw and a simple bun. Later, I found that R. O.'s was already selling a slaw burger. It is very good, I found, but the slaw is even better with barbecue!

In those days, before interstates connected Charlotte and Raleigh, Highway 64 was the usual route between the two cities. There you would find the Blue Mist, the must-stop barbecue restaurant outside Asheboro. The barbecue sandwiches were always good, and I always ran into friends traveling the same roads. With its closure a few years ago, travelers lost an icon.

In my three political campaigns, I was more successful at finding great gathering places for breakfast and lunch with supporters than I was at winning elections. At eateries such as Troutman's in Concord and Hussey's in Burlington, the reminders of visits by famous politicians make them mini-museums as well as good places to eat with the locals.

When I moved to Chapel Hill to work for University of North Carolina system president Dick Spangler, he introduced me to Breadmen's, where the great and bountiful servings of solid food and the ever-presence of policemen and community leaders made it my second home until my wife joined me in Chapel Hill. Now, she and I take our grandchildren there and spoil them with pancakes and French fries while we still split the giant vegetable plate, almost always choosing their tasty banana pudding, which Breadmen's includes as one of the veggie options, even though everybody knows it's not a vegetable. But I wanted to know about other country cooking places. Jack Hunt, a powerful legislator from Cleveland County, was married to a cousin of President Spangler, who told me I could go to Jack if I ever needed help in my work with the legislature. So one day I did ask him for help: "Where is the best place to get country cooking around here?"

He paused, squinted, smiled a little bit, and finally said, "Well, the truth is there is nothing better, I think, than Ruby's cooking." His wife, Spangler's cousin, is the Ruby in question. Jack and Ruby regularly invited their government friends for informal suppers of country ham, baked chicken, cornbread, biscuits with sourwood honey and molasses, and vegetables from her garden, including corn frozen minutes after it was picked the previous summer. There were always desserts of homemade cakes and pies. Of course, there was also the opportunity to make friends with governors, Supreme Court justices, and legislative leaders.

Once, when President Spangler and Governor Jim Hunt were at loggerheads about the governor's budget proposals for the university, they could hardly speak to each other until Jack invited them to breakfast with Ruby. Neither the governor nor the university president could say no to Ruby. It only was after they sat down to Ruby's cooking and warm spirit that they worked out a compromise.

Some of the other lobbyists had resources to entertain legislators at fancy and expensive restaurants. I had no expense account. But I found that I could always get wonderful and inexpensive country cooking and run into important legislators at places such as Big Daddy's and Finch's, where the food was great, the servers were friendly, and the atmosphere was warm and inclusive enough to be conducive to building trust.

On one occasion, university vice president Bill McCoy and I left from Chapel Hill about noon driving to Cullowhee for a meeting at Western Carolina University. By the time we were approaching Winston-Salem on I-40, McCoy said he was getting hungry for a barbecue sandwich. I quickly agreed but admitted that I did not know where there was a good place to stop. We called the law offices of the late Ham Horton, then serving in the legislature and a well-known food fan. Horton was unavailable, his receptionist told us, because he was in an important real estate closing.

"Tell him we only need him for a minute because we need a place to eat," we pled. Thankfully, Horton came to the phone and quickly gave us a recommendation and directions.

At that moment I knew that interstate travelers needed some sort of guidebook to the barbecue joints and country cooking places where the locals eat. I began to write about my favorite country cooking places in my weekly newspaper column. My readers like those columns better than my usual ones about politics and books. When I invited them to write about their favorite places, I got enough material for more columns and for a series of magazine articles that featured some of my favorites.

I left the university in the fall of 1997 to run for the U.S. Senate. After I was soundly defeated in the primary by John Edwards, Chancellor Joseph Oxendine at UNC-Pembroke asked me to work for him for six months. While I was there, he introduced me to Lumbee Indian culture and two of his favorite restaurants: Linda's, where the lunchtime crowd of locals politely welcomed the "university crowd" to join them for lunch, and Shef's, where the seafood suppers drew people from all over Lumbee Land.

A few months after that assignment ended, North Carolina Central University chancellor Julius Chambers asked me to work for him for a few months. I enjoyed eating with my staff at the faculty cafeteria; it was not a regular restaurant, of course, but the country food was delicious. One day the special plate was pigs' feet. I remember how everybody looked over to see how I was going to deal with that dish. I pretended that I did not notice their looks and cleaned my plate and ate all the meat and tasty fat from every toe.

Folks at Central introduced me to Dillard's, where people from all over Durham gathered to enjoy barbecue with a mustard-based sauce more like they serve in South Carolina. Sadly, Dillard's closed a few years ago. While in Durham, I met some of my Central staff at Bullock's in Durham as described later in this book.

Meanwhile, another interim job with the Trust for Public Land took me back to Charlotte for more than a year. I introduced my staff to Open Kitchen, which was the same as it was so many years earlier. They introduced me to Lupe's, where we gathered for simple but tasty fare and the chance to meet people from all over town. Both these great places are described in this book. But, unfortunately, another of my Charlotte favorites, Anderson's, home of The World's Best Pecan Pie and where I spent many happy mornings at business, political, church, and social gatherings, closed a few years ago.

But that is the challenge of writing about restaurants: even if we wish they would, they don't last forever. They go out of business, trade hands and change, or keep chugging until they run their natural course. But part of the joy in all these jobs I've had over the years and all the traveling I've done is finding new and welcoming places to pull up, get a sweet tea, and meet good folks while eating wonderful North Carolina home cooking.

I've written for years about these places, published books and countless columns about them and the people in them: from little diners with hushpuppies you never forget to watching people settle political differences over a slice of lemon pie, I've seen and tasted nearly everything. I love this state and love traveling its roads, finding what I find, and reporting back to you. I hope you enjoy what's ahead in this book and that it inspires you to go a little out of your way to find something special, where the folks will likely greet you like an old friend, even if it's your first visit.

INTERSTATE **26**

In one of the most beautiful sections of our state, this highway runs from the mountain border with eastern Tennessee through Asheville, Hendersonville, and Saluda and then down to the South Carolina line. I-26 opens the door for its travelers to make a quick visit to an eatery in a mountain holler or a small college town or other mountain towns where tourists and local mountain people sit down together for good, solid meals.

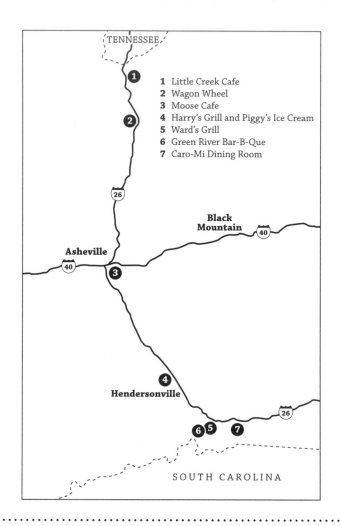

1 Little Creek Cafe
2 Wagon Wheel
3 Moose Cafe
4 Harry's Grill and Piggy's Ice Cream
5 Ward's Grill
6 Green River Bar-B-Que
7 Caro-Mi Dining Room

TENNESSEE

Black Mountain

Asheville

Hendersonville

SOUTH CAROLINA

Little Creek Cafe

1660 US 23, Mars Hill, NC 28754 · (828) 689-2307
Open for breakfast and lunch, except on Sunday

"She could flat make biscuits," says Shelia Kay Adams, famous local writer and musician, as she remembers the home cooking of the late Edna Boone, who ran Little Creek Cafe for 43 years and whose family still owns the building. Every subsequent owner has attempted to keep up and build on Edna Boone's legacy by baking biscuits and offering full breakfast options to draw crowds of locals and, in the summer, visitors from the nearby Wolf Laurel resort. And when I last tasted the biscuits at Little Creek, I was sure that Edna Boone would approve of her successors' efforts.

FROM I-26 Take Exit 3 to US 23A and turn left onto US 23A. Little Creek is just ahead on the right.

· ·

Wagon Wheel

89 Carl Eller Road, Mars Hill, NC 28754 · (828) 689-4755
Monday–Friday 6:00 A.M.–8:00 P.M.; Saturday 6:00 A.M.–2:00 P.M.

For more than 10 years, Wagon Wheel owner Camille Metcalf has been serving breakfast, lunch, and supper to her regular customers in Mars Hill—and to tourists. She gives them a hearty breakfast, lunch specials with everything included for about $6, and dinner for well under $10. And for the kids and college students there are always burgers, fries, and homemade pies.

FROM I-26 Take Exit 11 and follow NC 213 toward Mars Hill for about 1 mile. Wagon Wheel is on the left.

AFTER EATING Take a walk on the lovely campus of Mars Hill College. Some of the action in Ron Rash's novel *The Cove* is set in the town and on the campus during World War I. Rash was asked once why North Carolina produces so many good authors and so many good stories. He said, "This is what North Carolinians do. We do barbecue and novels."

Other nearby eateries are described in the I-40 chapter, including Little Pigs Bar-B-Q, Luella's Bar-B-Que, and 12 Bones Smokehouse.

Moose Cafe

570 Brevard Road #3, Asheville, NC 28806 · (828) 255-0920
Monday–Sunday 7:00 A.M.–8:00 P.M.
eatatthemoosecafe.com

It is always a great thing to hear about other people's favorite gathering and eating places. Sandra Arscott wrote to tell me about the Moose Cafe near the Farmers Market in Asheville. She bragged about the homemade biscuits and cornbread. She loves the Moose Cafe's apple butter so much that she always buys jars of it to take home. She told me about the iced tea served in Mason jars. She wrote about the great mountain views from the restaurant's windows, including a wonderful look at the Biltmore Hotel.

Based on her recommendation, I persuaded my Asheville friend John Curry to eat supper with me there. He ordered one of the special meat-and-two-vegetables plates. "It's delicious," he said, "but it's too much. I can't eat it all." Because I was hungry from a mountain hike, I ordered the "Country Feast." It costs a few dollars more but allowed me to order all the meat and vegetables I could eat, plus dessert. Just to be sure that their mashed potatoes, cabbage, collards, carrots, pinto beans, and other vegetables were as "Farmers Market fresh" as Sandra Arscott promised, I sampled them all. And Sandra was right. They were fresh and cooked "just right."

I asked John Curry a question I always raise on my search for eateries: "Is the restaurant a community gathering place, where local people come to meet and catch up with their friends?" John nodded, smiled, and pointed across the way to his friends Doug and Laura Manofsky, who were eating supper with two of their children. "Oh, yes, it's a place where all kinds of Asheville folks come," Doug said. "We got started a few years ago when the contractor who was building our new home recommended the Moose Cafe. We've been eating here regularly ever since."

If I lived in Asheville, I would be eating there regularly, too. Instead, I will have to wait until the next time I am traveling nearby. But I will not have to wait until then to sample some of the Moose's

*Moose Cafe
in Asheville*

best food. On the way out, John Curry and I stopped at the small gift shop inside the café. We studied the selection of T-shirts and souvenirs and were tempted by the handmade pottery, blankets, and rocking chairs that nearby mountain craftspeople leave for the Moose to display and sell. But like Sandra Arscott had written me, the gift shop's most popular item is Moose's apple butter, and John Curry bought me a couple of jars to take home and enjoy until I am back on I-26 again.

FROM I-26 Take Exit 33 (NC 191 North/Brevard Rd.). Follow Brevard Rd. north toward Asheville and the Farmers Market for 1.5 miles. The Moose Cafe is on the right just before you reach the Farmers Market.

FROM I-40 Take Exit 47 and follow signs to the Farmers Market.

AFTER EATING Wander in the restaurant's store for the apple butter and other gift ideas. Then find your way to the nearby Farmers Market to see what is in season.

....

Harry's Grill and
Piggy's Ice Cream

102 Duncan Hill Road, Hendersonville, NC 28792 · (828) 693-3726
Monday–Saturday 10:30 A.M.–8:00 P.M.;
Sunday (Piggy's Ice Cream only in summer) 1:00 P.M.–9:00 P.M.
www.harrysandpiggys.com

What are an ice cream shop and a grill doing under the same roof? I asked myself that question as I stood in line to place my order at Harry's Grill and looked across the way at a separate line of folks waiting to order ice cream at Piggy's.

I sat down in one of the booths and began to examine the items hanging on the walls all around—signs from Howard Johnson's, Wall Drug in South Dakota, and an old Esso station. There were Ronald McDonald and Big Boy statues. License tags from across the country, pictures, and all sorts of memorabilia covered every inch of the surrounding walls. Just what is going on here? I wondered again. It did not take me long to find the answer.

Mrs. "Piggy" Thompson, the owner of Harry's, Piggy's, and all the statues and signs on the wall, sat down at my booth and answered all my questions. "Back in 1980, when my late husband, Harry, told me he was going to start an ice cream stand here, I told him that I sure was not going to run it. But, when it was time to open up, Harry was still working at his regular job, and there was no one else to run it. So guess what? I came down here and started dipping ice cream, by myself—just like I said I would not do. We started with more than 20 flavors of Biltmore ice cream. Business gradually grew and grew. We did so well that pretty soon Harry decided he wanted to start a restaurant right here in the same place. Harry died while the restaurant's addition was still under construction. But we opened it in 1993 and, of course, named it after him. My sons Jeff and Todd are helping me now. In fact, they are doing most everything. Another son, Michael, who is a lawyer in Hendersonville, still comes by every now and then to help us dip ice cream. We are really proud of our barbecue. We smoke it with wood, and we offer a tomato-based sauce that we think is real good. We do have just one customer who says our barbecue is the best, but he brings his own sauce."

Piggy Thompson noticed that I was looking at a Howdy Doody figure on the wall. "Buffalo Bob himself once came by to buy ice cream and autographed it for us," she explained. "We've had some other celebrities to drop by. When I heard Perry Como had a place in Saluda, I invited him to come by for some ice cream, complimentary of course. But guess what? When he came, I wasn't here and the girls at the counter charged him for it just like everyone else. They didn't know who he was. That was hard for me to believe."

She told me that although the business increases in the summer, with tourists and lots of visits from the summer camps in the area, about 75 percent of their customers are always local. "We never did any advertising," she said. "Never needed to." Even if the barbecue and ice cream were not so good and the memorabilia on the walls was not so interesting, I would come back here just to have another visit with Piggy Thompson.

FROM I-26 Take Exit 49 (US 64 West/Hendersonville). Follow US 64 West toward Hendersonville for about 1 mile until it intersects with Dana Rd. Turn right on Dana Rd. (which becomes Duncan Hill Rd.). Go about one block, and after crossing East Seventh Ave., you will see Harry's and Piggy's on the right. They are across Duncan Hill Rd. from Lowe's.

AFTER EATING Just down the street, at 235 Duncan Hill Rd., is the Music Academy of Western North Carolina. Give them a call at (828) 693-3726 to let them know you are coming and maybe they will be able to show you some of their highly praised facilities.

Ward's Grill

24 Main Street, Saluda, NC 28773 · (828) 749-2321
Monday–Friday 6:30 A.M.–3:00 P.M.;
Saturday 6:00 A.M.–3:00 P.M.; closed Sunday
thompsons-store.com

Even if you're not hungry for home cooking, you should stop in Saluda, one of North Carolina's most charming small towns and just a couple of miles off the interstate. Saluda is the home of the Orchard Inn, one of the finest bed-and-breakfasts I have ever visited. The Purple Onion Cafe and Coffee House on Main Street is a favorite of mine—but not for home cooking. It has an upscale California-type menu, with modest North Carolina prices.

But if you want a country cooking breakfast or lunch, surrounded by old-time local people, take a walk down Main Street and stop at Ward's Grill. On my last visit, while I was sitting at one of its small tables sipping a cup of coffee with my hamburger "all the way," I thought for a moment that I had been transported back in time about 50 years.

Current owner Clark Thompson explained how the history of Ward's Grill goes back a long way. George Lafatte Thompson first opened Thompson's Store in Saluda in 1890, which makes it the oldest grocery store still in existence in North Carolina. His daughter, Lola Thompson Ward, took over the store from her father in the late 1930s. Husband Roy Ward encouraged her to open the grill next door in 1960, which became the Ward's Grill we know today.

Charlie Ward, one of their sons, created the recipe for his famous "Charlie's Sage Sausage" in the 1940s. It is still made fresh daily, using the same recipe and sausage grinder for more than 75 years. The sausage is served in the grill as well as sold in the store's meat market. After declining health forced Charlie to sell the two businesses in 2008 and a short period of ownership by others, current owner Clark Thompson stepped in. Clark explained, "Charlie's widow, Judy, and I teamed up to bring the store and grill back into the family, reopening the grill in July 2010 and Thompson's Store in January 2011. Judy is a minor business partner and manager for the store. Melissa Wood, who had run her own grill in a nearby community for ten years, manages the grill."

I still remember the hamburger from my visit, as I looked up at the high ceilings, listened to the onions sizzling on the grill, and thought to myself that this was a better look at times gone by than any museum could ever provide.

Charlie was right. The fresh meat from Thompson's next door gave my hamburger a good start. But it was the chili Charlie bragged about that made the whole thing a perfect treat. But Clark Thompson says they have gone one better. "One very popular addition to Ward's Grill menu is our CJ burger which is a 50-50 mixture of our own Charlie's Famous Sage Sausage and fresh ground chuck. Customers love them. And at lunch Melissa's cornbread salad, cold slaw, potato salad, tuna salad, and cobblers are also more than worthy of writing home about."

FROM I-26 Take Exit 59 (Saluda) and follow the signs toward Saluda, traveling Louisiana Ave. (Ozone Rd.) for 1 mile to US 176. Turn right on US 176 (Main St.), then go a half-mile into Saluda.

AFTER EATING Visit the historic Thompson's Store next door, open daily from 8:00 A.M. until 6:00 P.M. (6:30 on Saturday) and on Sunday from 11:00 A.M. to 4:00 P.M. during the summer.

. . . .

Green River Bar-B-Que

131 US 176, Saluda, NC 28773 · (828) 749-9892
Monday 11:00 A.M.–8:00 P.M.;
Tuesday–Saturday 11:00 A.M.–8:00 P.M.;
Sunday 12:00 P.M.–8:00 P.M.
greenriverbbq.com

For almost 25 years, Melanie Talbot has been serving Eastern-style North Carolina barbecue to western North Carolinians. And they love it. Along with a small pork plate for about $10, she will give you three sides, including, if you want, some that you will not find other places, like tomato pie, Vidalia onion slaw, sweet potato fries, or corn nuggets with creamed corn in the middle. No wonder it is a popular gathering place for Saluda residents and tourists from all over.

FROM I-26 Take Exit 59 and follow the signs to Saluda, traveling Louisiana Ave. (Ozone Rd.) for 1 mile to US 176. Turn right on US 176 (Main St.) into Saluda, and just over the bridge Green River will be on your left.

AFTER EATING Make your way back to Main St. and explore the town's history of the railroad over the years.

. . . .

Caro-Mi Dining Room

3231 US 176, Tryon, NC 28782 · (828) 859-5200
Wednesday–Saturday 5:00 P.M.–about 8:00 P.M.;
closed Sunday–Tuesday
MAY NOT ACCEPT CREDIT CARDS
caro-mi.com

On the porch of the Caro-Mi just outside Tryon, you can wait for a wonderful meal while listening to the rushing sounds of the Pacolet River as it flows by. Charles Stafford, a former teacher and school administrsator, has owned Caro-Mi since 1990. He is proud that two of North Carolina's leading food experts tout his restaurant—for different reasons.

Jim Early, author of *The Best Tar Heel Barbecue: Manteo to Murphy*, raves about the skillet-fried chicken livers and mountain trout, along with the vinegar-based shredded coleslaw.

Bob Garner, of UNC-TV and *Our State* magazine fame, recommends especially the old-fashioned, North Carolina, "climate cured" country ham served here. Other friends also tell me about the country ham that the owners call "The Ham What Am."

FROM I-26 Take Exit 67 (NC 108/Tryon). Follow NC 108 toward Tryon for 2.3 miles until it meets Harmon Field Rd. Bear right and follow Harmon Field Rd. for 0.7 mile, where it intersects with US 176. Turn right on US 176 and follow it for about 2 miles. Caro-Mi is on the left.

AFTER EATING Sit on the porch of the Caro-Mi and listen to the rushing sounds of the North Pacolet River flowing by, on its way to South Carolina and the Broad and Santee Rivers and the Atlantic Ocean. There are different stories about the source of the Pacolet name. Some say it means "swift horse" in Cherokee. Others say it means "swift messenger" in French. The logo of the former Pacolet Mills in South Carolina featured a "swift horse."

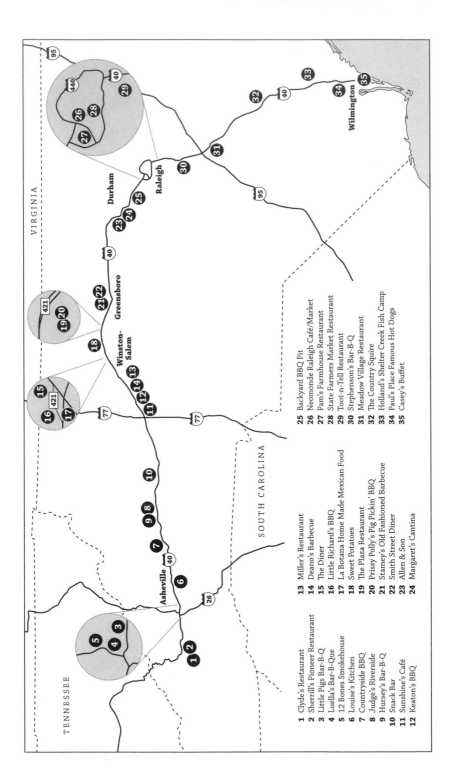

VIRGINIA

TENNESSEE

SOUTH CAROLINA

Wilmington

Raleigh

Durham

Winston-Salem

Greensboro

Asheville

95
440
40
29
33
32
40
34
35
26
28
27
30
31
95
25
24
23
40
22
21
19
20
18
421
15
16
17
13
14
12
11
77
77
10
9
8
7
40
6
26
3
5
4
1
2

1 Clyde's Restaurant
2 Sherrill's Pioneer Restaurant
3 Little Pigs Bar-B-Q
4 Luella's Bar-B-Que
5 12 Bones Smokehouse
6 Louise's Kitchen
7 Countryside BBQ
8 Judge's Riverside
9 Hursey's Bar-B-Q
10 Snack Bar
11 Sunshine's Café
12 Keaton's BBQ

13 Miller's Restaurant
14 Deano's Barbecue
15 The Diner
16 Little Richard's BBQ
17 La Botana Home Made Mexican Food
18 Sweet Potatoes
19 The Plaza Restaurant
20 Prissy Polly's Pig Pickin' BBQ
21 Stamey's Old Fashioned Barbecue
22 Smith Street Diner
23 Allen & Son
24 Margaret's Cantina

25 Backyard BBQ Pit
26 Neomonde Raleigh Café/Market
27 Pam's Farmhouse Restaurant
28 State Farmers Market Restaurant
29 Toot-n-Tell Restaurant
30 Stephenson's Bar-B-Q
31 Meadow Village Restaurant
32 The Country Squire
33 Holland's Shelter Creek Fish Camp
34 Paul's Place Famous Hot Dogs
35 Casey's Buffet

INTERSTATE 40

I guess driving from the eastern part of the state to the mountains these days is a lot better than it used to be.

After all, instead of driving on the curvy two-lane roads that took us through Valdese, Morganton, Marion, and Old Fort, we just drive along four-lane I-40. And if there are no traffic jams or closed highways, we can just cruise along the entire way without stopping.

Well, maybe it's better than it used to be, maybe it's not. Come to think of it, I enjoyed some of the times on those old highways, riding through these mountain towns and sometimes stopping to eat a real meal in a local restaurant.

Today, locally owned, home cooking restaurants are harder to find on I-40 than a bend in the road. But if you are like me and love to find the kinds of places where the owners and serving staff make you feel like you belong there, read on. I have found a few good places to stop on your next trip to the mountains.

Most North Carolinians know that you can travel from Wilmington to California without hitting a stoplight if you stay on I-40. But if you are leaving North Carolina for California or other points west, you ought not to go without having a meal in the company of some real North Carolinians. If you are traveling west of Asheville, keep reading, because I have found some great spots for home cooking that will help you remember our state until you return.

Following the 420 miles of I-40 that take you from the Tennessee line to Wilmington, you can visit every region of our state and drive by most of its major cities. You will also have the opportunity to eat the same barbecue Barack Obama did, to find it cooked and sauced many different ways in addition to the Lexington and Eastern styles, and to be amazed at the bountiful all-you-can eat buffets in eastern North Carolina's rural communities. It is a long drive, so take a break along the way and enjoy the food and fellowship at one of the places I have found for you along I-40.

....

Clyde's Restaurant

2107 South Main Street, Waynesville, NC 28786
Tuesday–Sunday 6:00 A.M.–9:00 P.M.; closed Monday

Clyde's is a favorite memory of novelist and expert on perfumes Sarah Colton, a native of Asheville who now lives in Paris, where she still thinks about the chocolate pie she ate at Clyde's growing up. It is still on the menu. Others say the lemon pie is even better. In its "Best Kept Secrets," series, The *News and Observer* compared Clyde's with a fancier restaurant and wrote, "We were happier with the fare at Clyde's Restaurant, a bustling comfort-food diner. Pretty good fried chicken, mac and cheese, and a generous salad."

Clyde's is about 10 miles from I-40, but it may be your last chance (or first opportunity) to get North Carolina home cooking on the way to or from the Tennessee line.

FROM I-40 Take Exit 27 (US 19-23 South) toward Waynesville for about 10 miles into Waynesville. Take Exit 98 and turn left onto Hyatt Creek Rd. and then immediately take a left onto South Main St.

AFTER EATING Follow South Main St. into the center of Waynesville, which was the model for the town of Cold Mountain in Charles Frazier's novel.

Sherrill's Pioneer Restaurant

8363 Carolina Boulevard, Clyde, NC 28721 · (828) 627-9880
Monday–Saturday 5:00 A.M.–8:00 P.M.; closed Sunday

Dean Sherrill's family has been running the Pioneer for as long as anybody can remember. Always a family affair, Dean, his brother, and their mother operated it for many years. More recently, Dean Sherrill and his wife, Lisa, have run the Pioneer with the help of a lot of family members. Now their children are taking charge.

Local folks crowd into the small restaurant and fill its 10 booths and all the counter space for breakfast and lunch. Travelers experience a trip back in time to the America of the 1950s. They see signs on the wall like "If we don't take care of our customer . . . somebody else will." Try the homemade vegetable beef soup, a bargain. At lunch and dinner, locals love the meat-and-three-vegetables specials.

FROM I-40 Take Exit 27 (connector to US 19-23-74). Continue for about 1.5 miles. Then bear left and follow signs to US 19-23 North into Clyde, which becomes Carolina Blvd. Sherrill's is on the right.

AFTER EATING Drive a few blocks to get a look at the Pigeon River (named for the extinct passenger pigeons that used the river to guide their migration). Or make your way into downtown Clyde and visit stores like Old Grouch's Military Surplus, which the Veteran-Owned Business organization says "is the largest, most knowledgeable and best stocked military surplus store in Western North Carolina. A real, traditional military surplus store with actual military surplus." You can check out the store's stock in advance at store.oldgrouch.biz.

Another nearby eatery is described in the
I-26 chapter, the Moose Cafe.

Little Pigs Bar-B-Q

384 McDowell Street, Asheville, NC 28803 · (828) 254-4253
Monday–Saturday 10:30 A.M.–8:00 P.M.; closed Sunday
littlepigsbbq.net

Our friends Margie and Tom Haber live in Chapel Hill now, and they know something about fine dining in expensive restaurants. Their nephew, Hunter Lewis, has been a writer and editor at *Bon Appétit*, *Southern Living*, and *Cooking Light*. But they grew up in Asheville, and their eyes get a little misty when they talk about Little Pigs Bar-B-Q in their hometown. "It has been around since we were teenagers and it was just up the street from Lee H. Edwards High School (now Asheville High School) and that is where all the high school kids went after school. And the Swicegoods are still there, aren't they?"

Peggy and Joe Swicegood have been together for more than 60 years, counting courtship and marriage. Both still come to work every day to help their managers, Bruce Gordon and Matt Thomas. Joe works the lines to make sure his customers are happy even when they have to wait.

Although the barbecue is still the main draw and they cook 60 to 70 pork shoulders every week, the pressure-fried or broasted chicken is also very tasty and very popular. After eating several pieces, *Cold Mountain* author Charles Frazier said that he was taking Little Pigs' chicken to his next Inman family reunion.

FROM I-40 Take Exit 50 toward US 25 North. Follow US 25 North (Hendersonville Rd., All Souls Crescent St., and McDowell St.) for about 2 miles. Little Pigs is on the right.

AFTER EATING Cross the street and walk on the campus of historic Asheville High School. Its alumni, in addition to the Habers, include famed UNC and professional football player Charlie Justice and noted author Marisha Pessl, who appeared recently on UNC-TV's *North Carolina Bookwatch*.

Luella's Bar-B-Que

501 Merrimon Avenue, Asheville, NC 28804 · (828) 505-7427
Monday–Thursday 11:00 A.M.–9:00 P.M.;
Friday–Saturday 11:00 A.M.–10:00 P.M.; Sunday 12:00 P.M.–9:00 P.M.
luellasbbq.com

Katherine Frazier and her husband, Charles, introduced me to Luella's, one of their favorites. Maybe they like it so much because Luella's treasures its history and family connections. Owner and "pit boss" Jeff Miller explains that the restaurant is named after his grandmother, who "did all the cooking when the family would get together for Sunday dinner and holidays. Scratch cooking from the garden at its best. What she handed down was an understanding of how great food is created—honest good cooking, made with a loving hand." Jeff tries to follow that tradition, using local foods and giving a variety of options in addition to his highly praised barbecue. Or, as he brags, "Made from scratch, high quality grub, tasting great every day."

At lunchtime, one patron, Brian Ross, bragged about the wings ("smoked for two hours and fried") and the ribs and "the Bloody Marys on Sundays." Customer Kate Ross told me she prefers the simple salad with a little chicken on top. It is not a fancy place, but the wood paneling gives it a comfortable feel. Locals love it, and sometimes it gets crowded. At lunch, customers place orders at the counter; at supper, it is table service.

FROM I-40 Take I-240 into Asheville (at Exit 46 or Exit 53).

FROM I-240 Take Exit 5A and turn right to follow Merrimon Ave. for 1 mile. Luella's is on the right.

AFTER EATING If you're in the mood for dessert, YoLo, which serves locally sourced frozen yogurt and toppings, is right across the parking lot. In the daytime, take a walk on the Weaver Park Trail that begins just around the corner.

Jeff Miller of Luella's Bar-B-Que in Asheville (photo by Mike Belleme)

12 Bones Smokehouse

5 Riverside Drive, Asheville, NC 28801 · (828) 253-4499
Monday–Friday 11:00 A.M.–4:00 P.M.; closed Saturday–Sunday
www.12bones.com

Even if 12 Bones had not been made famous by Barack Obama's visits there, it would be a "must-do" in Asheville. Thomas Montgomery and Sabra Kelly opened 12 Bones in the Riverside area in 2005. In 2012 they sold the restaurant to Bryan King and Angela Koh King, who have continued the reputation for making everything from scratch. Bryan grew up in Spruce Pine and Asheville. After college at North Carolina State and travel in Asia, he moved to San Francisco, where he met Angela, who grew up in Iowa. Her father escaped from North Korea as a child, which is a story in itself. When 12 Bones went on the market, Angela and Bryan moved to Asheville, learned every position in 12 Bones, and have continued its success. Now, as experienced operators, they say, "We believe that simple ingredients and lots of care in preparation make the best food."

When my group visited, John Curry got a vegetable plate with baked beans, corn pudding, and collards. The rest of us feasted on the signature 12-boned ribs, delicious and addictive, smoked with cherry wood coals. Other dishes set 12 Bones apart from the usual North Carolina barbecue, but the ribs are very special.

One reason to hurry your visit: 12 Bones and its humble one-story building could be jeopardized by a riverfront redevelopment plan. Bryan and Angela plan to continue 12 Bones even if it has to move. They also do a booming business at their Arden location at 3578 Sweeten Creek Rd.

FROM I-40 Take I-240 into Asheville (at Exit 46 or Exit 53).

FROM I-240 *If headed east:* Take Exit 3B toward Westgate, then turn right onto Craven Connector. Follow that road for 1 mile and make a hard left to stay on Craven Connector, which immediately dead-ends. Turn left onto Hazel Mill Rd. for 200 yards. Turn left onto Craven St. for 0.2 mile, and then turn right onto Riverside Dr.

If headed west: Take Exit 4A for US 19 North/US 23 North/US 70 West/I-26 toward Weaverville/Woodfin. Stay right and immediately take the Hill St. exit, and then follow Hill St. to Riverside Dr. Turn left and follow Riverside Dr. for 1 mile; 12 Bones will be on the right.

AFTER EATING Take a stroll through the surrounding River Arts District and visit art and craft studios (find more at www.ashevillerad.com), or take a few minutes to watch the French Broad drift by from the edge of the 12 Bones parking lot.

. . . .

Louise's Kitchen

115 Black Mountain Avenue, Black Mountain, NC 28711
(828) 357-5446
Monday–Saturday 7:30 A.M.–2:00 P.M.;
Sunday brunch 10:00 A.M.–2:00 P.M.
www.louisesblackmtn.com

Louise's is a favorite of Doug Orr, president emeritus of nearby Warren Wilson College and coauthor with Fiona Ritchie of *Wayfaring Strangers: The Musical Voyage from Scotland and Ulster to Appalachia*. Doug and his wife, Darcy, brag about the "wide variety of breakfast items (the blueberry waffles are a favorite) and lunch items such as Big Boy Burritos and Smoked Pork Quesadillas."

Twice a month at Louise's, Doug meets with "a little collection of retired doctors, college presidents and Presbyterian ministers," and it is the place where Scotland's Fiona Ritchie, host of NPR's *Thistle and Shamrock*, eats when she visits the region for the annual Swannanoa Gathering of folk music performances and workshops.

The owners, Bud and Charissa Rainey, converted the white-framed building for restaurant use. Built in 1904 as private residence and known as the Stepp House, it is the oldest surviving building within the village of Black Mountain.

FROM I-40 Take Exit 64 onto Broadway toward Black Mountain. Go 0.5 mile. Turn left on Terry Estate Dr. and go 0.2 mile. Turn right on Black Mountain Ave. and go 0.2 mile. Louise's is on the right.

....

Countryside BBQ

2070 Rutherford Road, Marion, NC 28752 · (828) 652-4885
Monday–Thursday 11:00 A.M.–9:00 P.M.;
Friday–Saturday 6:30 A.M.–9:00 P.M.; Sunday 11:00 A.M.–3:00 P.M.
www.countrysidebbq.net

If you're willing to weave around a few winding roads, there is a good payoff to be found at Countryside BBQ. Tasty salads and sandwiches, including a good barbecue sandwich, a local favorite, are part of a diverse menu with daily specials and a Sunday buffet.

The side dishes, which they call "country sides" (collard greens, fried okra, sweet potatoes, and green beans), are prepared southern-style. Get four of them on a vegetable plate for less than $7.

On Friday and Saturday mornings, you will find a crowd starting the day with a breakfast special of a country ham biscuit and baked cinnamon apples. Owners Rob Noyes and David Ditt are natives of Marion and have years of restaurant experience. They acquired the restaurant from longtime owners Gary and Lanetta Byrd in 2006. Countryside proudly reports that "President Obama and his team stopped by on their tour of North Carolina, and we were happy to provide them with the best of southern hospitality and catering!"

FROM I-40 Take Exit 86 (NC 226). From the intersection, head north on NC 226 toward Marion. Go 1 mile until NC 226 intersects with US 221. Turn right onto US 221 (Rutherford Rd.) and go about one-half mile. Countryside is on the left.

AFTER EATING Enjoy the small-town allure of the front porch in one of the "sit-and-chat" white rocking chairs. Or drive a few blocks to Fabulous Finds and Gifts at 1790 Rutherford Rd. to see if there is a treasure there for you. If you would like to walk away some of the good meal, the Peavine Trail begins nearby. Head north on Rutherford Rd. for about 0.5 mile to Ford Way. Turn right, and the trail begins on the left near the intersection with Glenwood Ave. This railroad corridor trail goes 1.5 miles to State St. in downtown Marion.

· ·

Judge's Riverside

128 Greenlee Ford Road, Morganton, NC 28655 · (828) 433-5798
Sunday–Thursday 11:00 A.M.–9:00 P.M.;
Friday–Saturday 11:00 A.M.–10:00 P.M.;
closes an hour earlier in winter
www.judgesriverside.com

Some people still call this restaurant Judge's Barbecue; but its current name, Judge's Riverside, reflects a new ambience, and the menu is fancier, too. They will even let you take it home as a souvenir. Judge's offers great food, including barbecue sandwiches (both chopped pork and Texas-style beef) and seafood dishes.

Worth a side trip every time, the restaurant sits above one of the few places where the Catawba River still flows freely. You can sit on porches that overlook the river. I don't know of any other place this close to one of our interstates where you can get a good meal and enjoy such a nice setting.

FROM I-40 Take Exit 103 and head north on US 64. Go 1 mile to Flemming Dr. Turn left, and go 1 mile to the intersection with US 70. Turn left, and go 0.5 mile. Turn right onto Greenlee Ford Rd.

AFTER EATING Take a walk down to the river and stop for a while and listen to the Catawba go by. If you have time, go to the end of Greenlee Ford Rd. and take a walk or bike ride on the Catawba River Greenway, which meanders along the river for about 3 miles, to and through historic Morganton.

Hursey's Bar-B-Q

300 Carbon City Road, Morganton, NC 28655 · (828) 437-3001
Wednesday–Saturday 11:00 A.M.–8:00 P.M.;
closed Sunday–Tuesday

Years ago, I said to Mike Starnes, the owner of Hursey's in Morganton, "You know, I thought Hursey's was in Burlington." I had first found his place just a few minutes from I-40 and not far from Judge's Riverside.

"Well, you are almost right," Mike said. "I am the only franchisee of Hursey's. I worked with them in Burlington and learned how they cook. They let me use their name. I cook with wood just like they do. But I've had to make a few accommodations to local tastes, including having a tomato-based sauce for my customers."

Mike grew up in Charlotte and became a fan of barbecue all over the state. "I stopped in Shelby just the other day at one of the Bridges restaurants," he says, referencing the famous, though unrelated, barbecue joints just west of his hometown. "I just couldn't resist."

Mike opened his business in Morganton almost 25 years ago, and he has no plans to leave. He built a big pit where he cooks the barbecue with hickory wood coals just like Hursey's in Burlington. He and his wife home-schooled their four children, who were ages 4, 6, 8, and 10 when I first met them. The then-eight-year-old son, Cooper, told me that he was helping his dad in the restaurant. His dad told me that Cooper could mop the kitchen better than the regular employees. Time flies. Cooper went to UNC–Chapel Hill, following his older sister, Flora, there.

Mike's restaurant serves a fine barbecue plate. His round hushpuppies, fresh and crisp, were as good as I have ever eaten. His barbecue plate costs less than at most places. Barbecue is the specialty; but Mike says the local crowd also loves catfish and chicken, and he is happy to oblige.

If you're hungry for good Burlington-style barbecue, then

Morganton's Hursey's is worth the few extra minutes it takes to get there from the interstate.

Not much has changed since my first visit 15 years ago, except that Mike now closes on Sunday. "It's been good being able to go to church. Some of our good customers complain, but most understand and still support us," Mike said.

FROM I-40 Take Exit 103 (US 64/Morganton). From the intersection, head north on US 64 toward Morganton. Go about 1 mile to an intersection (Fleming Dr.). Turn left, following US 64. Go about 1 mile to the intersection of US 64 (Fleming Dr.) and US 70. Turn left and go west on US 70 about a mile. Hursey's is on the right.

AFTER EATING The Catawba River Trail is nearby. See a description under the entry for Judge's Riverside.

. . . .

Snack Bar

1346 1st Avenue SW, Hickory, NC 28602 · (828) 322-5432
Open every day, 6:00 A.M.–10:00 P.M.; closed Christmas Day

The first time I visited the Snack Bar, Glenda Young, one of the managers, showed me over to what she said was the Liars' Club table. "They talk about everything. Religion, politics, and even sex," she said. "But I tell them that is all they can do, just talk about it."

The members of the Liars' Club are mostly retired men, and they gather around a big table at the Snack Bar every morning about 6:30 for coffee and a little breakfast. They'll go home for a while after their meal and then return to the Liars' Club table for a little more coffee and conversation in the middle of the morning. Some of them go home for a while after coffee and come back for lunch, then come back for coffee in the afternoon, and then some of them come back for supper, sometimes bringing a spouse or friend.

On the day I visited, it seemed that all of Hickory had come to the Snack Bar for lunch. Men in short sleeves and ties were huddled over their meals with notebooks working on business deals. Groups of men and women taking a break from the office, truck drivers and construction workers, retired couples, and families filled the 200 seats.

The Snack Bar serves a variety of solid home cooking dishes—mostly meat-and-two-vegetables plates priced at about $8 or $10. But there is an added bonus: a salad and fruit buffet with soup for a modest price. That soup was hearty and thick with beef and vegetables and could have made a meal in itself. Tom Fitz, a retired physician, was eating lunch with his wife, Fran, their daughter, Wink Gaines, and her friend Mary Elizabeth Hardee. Dr. Fitz told me, "Someday, everybody in Hickory comes to the Snack Bar."

In 1946, Robert Frye opened the Snack Bar at its current location, with eleven stools at the counter and two tables. For many years, his daughter, Libby, and her husband, Eddie Yount, owned a greatly expanded restaurant. Their son, Brad Yount, now owns the business. According to manager Glenda Young, lots of the employees, particularly the waitresses, "have been here for a long time. The secret of success, I tell my waitresses, is to take the seven tables that I give each of them and build a business, their own business, around those seven tables. If they treat their customers right and get to know their names and their children's names, those customers will keep coming back to their seven tables. We're going to lose some of our best waitresses to retirement someday, and I am not sure how we're going to replace them. But right now, it is like a big family."

Some folks in Hickory call the Snack Bar the "Longview Country Club," after the nearby suburb. With the regular customers coming back to their usual tables, being served by waitresses who know their names, and being surrounded by their friends, no wonder they think of the Snack Bar as their own private club. I found that strangers are welcome, too. My waitress did not know my name, but she greeted me with a smile. Other customers nodded and smiled, too, indicating that they would welcome my questions and conversation.

"What would happen," I asked Glenda Young, "if I took a seat at the Liars' Club table?" "Oh, they would be glad," she replied. "But you had better be ready to take some kidding and give it back to them, because they sure do enjoy teasing each other and everybody else."

Next time I visit the Snack Bar, I plan to get up enough courage to get a temporary seat at the Liars' Club table. If you get there before I do and persuade them to let you sit with them for a few minutes, we will all declare you to be an Eatery Winner.

FROM I-40 Take Exit 123B (US 321 North toward Lenoir). Follow US 321, passing under US 70, for about 1.5 miles to the first stop-light. Here take a right onto Thirteenth St. Follow Thirteenth St. for two blocks until it dead-ends at First Ave. Turn left onto First Ave. Go about half a block and you will see the Snack Bar on the right.

Another nearby eatery, Carolina Bar-B-Q,
is described in the I-77 chapter.

· ·

Sunshine's Café

193 Crawford Road, Statesville, NC 28625 · (704) 873-1529
Monday–Friday 6:00 A.M.–3:00 P.M.; closed Saturday–Sunday

My friend Randy Gardner knows more about how to find quality home cooking near the big highways than anybody I know. So when he told me about Sunshine's, I knew I had to share the information with you. He wrote he'd passed by the place for 20 years before venturing inside, and he was glad he did. "They've been in business since 1985," he wrote me. "Good food. Excellent service. Family-owned. In addition to sandwiches, burgers, hot dogs, fish, etc., they have blue-plate specials with flounder, barbecue, and hamburger steak." Randy passed by all those things for a cheeseburger and a spaghetti plate. The cheeseburger is a favorite for many customers.

Another Sunshine's fan said it is like Mel's Diner in the old TV series *Alice*. Like Randy, I have driven by the nearby Davis Hospital on I-40 many times and never knew about Sunshine's. Just another reason it pays to have good friends.

When I finally made my way to Sunshine's, I was immediately overwhelmed by the sunshiny spirit of the owner, Hazel Craddock Pulliam. Run by Hazel and her husband, Walter; their son, Victor; and daughter, Wendy Czerkie, Sunshine's has been their family business since 1991. Walter and Hazel married more than 55 years ago, when Hazel was 15, she told me.

Their customers are like family, too. Wendy showed me a book that lists her regular customers' favorite dishes. "When beef liver is on the menu, which is not often, I know who to call, and he always comes in."

And when new customers come in, Hazel says she likes to welcome them and find out where they came from. She sure made me feel at home.

FROM I-40 Take Exit 154. Turn north onto Old Mocksville Rd. toward Davis Hospital for about 0.5 mile. Turn left onto Wilson Park Rd. and go 0.7 mile. Turn right onto Crawford Rd. Go 0.4 mile, and Sunshine's will be on the left.

Keaton's BBQ

17365 Cool Springs Road, Cleveland, NC 27013 · (704) 278-1619
Wednesday–Saturday 11:00 A.M.–2:00 P.M. and 5:00 P.M.–9:00 P.M.;
closed Sunday–Tuesday
MAY NOT ACCEPT CREDIT CARDS
www.keatonsoriginalbbq.com

I don't know how to say it other than this: Keaton's is something different—something you should not miss.

First of all, you have to drive around in the country for about 3 miles from the interstate intersection to get to Keaton's. But when you find it, there is nothing but Keaton's anywhere around. In other words, everybody who goes to Keaton's is simply going to Keaton's. They do not just "happen by."

Second, if you try the house specialty, fried barbecued chicken, you are going to have a delightful taste experience unlike anything you have ever had before. First, it's crispy fried, then dipped in Keaton's special sauce that blends with the crust and seeps into the meat.

Third, at Keaton's, things are done "their way." For instance, when I entered the cinderblock building and lined up behind the counter, I looked up at the menu on the wall. It told me that my order of fried barbecued chicken would come with a slice of white bread and nothing else. To get one of their side dishes, I would have to order and pay for it separately. When I ordered iced tea, they gave me a tray with a glass of tea and a pitcher to take to my seat. They gave me a number that was my table or booth assignment. I paid in cash, went to my assigned seat, and waited for an attendant to bring my fried barbecued chicken.

Keaton's is open when it wants to be—only four days a week, Wednesday through Saturday. So, why then, you ask, is Keaton's so popular? Why does it have a loyal following of locals—and out-of-towners who travel great distances to gather there? It is the special fried barbecued chicken dish, of course. Oh, boy, does it taste good. It is also the wonderful variety of people who work and eat there.

Then, too, there is the history. Local customer Jerry Cartner told me that he has been eating chicken and other dishes regularly at Keaton's for more than 30 years. In the old days, it was even more different, he said.

B. W. Keaton, who founded Keaton's around 1953, came from a nearby family of African American farmers. In the early days, according to Cartner, Keaton's was a very small building with a dirt floor. Locals dropped by to get Mr. Keaton's chicken and drink a beer. If anybody started to get rowdy, Mr. Keaton could keep things under control—everybody knew that he kept a shotgun under the counter.

"Keaton had a brother who always took the orders," Cartner said. "He never wrote any of them down and remembered everything perfectly. We tried to trick him by making the orders complicated, but we never could fool him." Keaton died in 1989. His niece, Kathleen Murray, and her son, David Dwayne Harris, run Keaton's now. The shotgun is gone, and the crowd is family oriented and very orderly. Still, it is one of the few "home cooking" places near the interstate where you can get a beer with your meal.

The clientele is decidedly mixed. On one of my visits, I met two sophisticated women decorators who now live in Toronto and Chicago. They were visiting their mother, who lives in Winston-Salem. "Don't use our names, but we bring our mother to Keaton's every time we come home." "How long does it take you all to get here from Winston-Salem?" I asked them. "Oh, that depends on how hungry we are," they said, laughing. "And we used to know some people who came down here regularly in a chauffeured Rolls-Royce. They would bring their silverware and cloth napkins with them."

If you find your way to Keaton's today, you'll likely see a parking lot crowded with pickup trucks rather than Rolls-Royces. But there may be a Lexus or two, which is good evidence that Keaton's special fried barbecued chicken still has fans from every station in life.

FROM I-40 Take Exit 162 (US 64 West). Follow US 64, heading west for about 1.5 miles to its intersection with Woodleaf Rd. You will see a Keaton's sign on the corner to the left. Turn left onto Woodleaf Rd. and follow it though rolling countryside for about 1.5 miles until you see Keaton's on the right. (Woodleaf Rd. changes into Cool Springs Rd. when you leave Iredell County and go into Rowan County about one-half mile before you reach Keaton's).

AFTER EATING How about a quick trip to Pittsburg? Follow Cool Springs Rd. about one-half mile, and where it intersects with Chenault/Steel/Dooley Rd. is a crossroads that Google Maps identifies as Pittsburg. Nothing is there other than a very nice church building. Warning: There is no mention of Pittsburg, N.C., in William Powell's *North Carolina Gazetteer*. But you can still say you have been there.

Miller's Restaurant

710 Wilkesboro Street, Mocksville, NC 27028 · (336) 751-2621
Monday–Thursday 5:00 A.M.–10:00 P.M.;
Friday 6:00 A.M.–11:00 P.M.; Saturday 6:00 A.M.–10:00 P.M.;
Sunday 7:00 A.M.–10:00 P.M.
www.millersrestaurant52.com

On the outside, Miller's Restaurant still looks like the same truck stop that Sheek Miller founded back in 1952 at the busy intersection of Highways 64 and 601. Although it's now a little bit off the beaten path, a few old truckers and some smart new ones still find their way to Miller's. But today it is more a community and family gathering place for folks in Mocksville.

On the inside, visitors from the 1950s would feel right at home. They could still sit at the same counter or choose a table in the dining room that has not changed much in 50 years. When I stopped for supper, the dining room was crowded with young families, retired couples, one or two truckers, and a few folks like me who came to eat alone. Friendly waitresses dressed in T-shirts and shorts kept busy serving us all. My waitress was a Miller cousin, and she told me that most of her coworkers had been there for "a long, long time." Sheek Miller would be proud of his son, Kip, the current owner. Kip runs the place the same way his dad did back in 1953.

I asked a woman who was eating there with her husband and three children why they came to Miller's. "We like it because we can get something for all of us here," she replied. "One of the kids had breakfast. Another had a meat-and-two-vegetables plate, and the rest of us had seafood. And it is all good."

Hungry for vegetables, I ordered fried squash, baked apples, and creamed potatoes. The vegetables tasted fresh and delicious. The round, crisp hushpuppies that came with them were good enough to compete with those at North Carolina's best barbecue restaurants. My waitress kept my iced tea glass full and gave me a big smile every time she passed by.

When she finally brought me a bill, I realized that I had filled myself up for just a few dollars. Even if the prices were not so reasonable and the food so good, I would be coming back to Miller's whenever I could, if only to take a trip back to the 1950s.

FROM I-40 Take Exit 170 (US 601/Mocksville). Follow US 601 for 1.5 miles. At a stoplight at the intersection with Wilkesboro St., turn left and go one block.

AFTER EATING Visit Joppa Cemetery, about 0.6 mile north on Yadkinville Rd, on the right. Daniel Boone's parents, Squire and Sarah Boone, are buried there.

· ·

Deano's Barbecue

140 N. Clement Street, Mocksville, NC 27028 · (336) 751-5820
Tuesday–Saturday 11:00 A.M.–8:00 P.M.; closed Sunday–Monday

Owner Dean Allen has been in the barbecue business since 1961. As a high school student, he worked as a curb boy for Buck's Barbecue restaurant, which he later bought and renamed Deano's. His long experience brings good results that have been praised by expert Jim Early, who says Deano's barbecue is "pound-the-table good."

Early says that the brown pieces mixed in the chopped meat "give each bite that pungent smoky taste that makes the flavor explode in your mouth." He continues, lyrically, that the sliced white meat from the shoulder of the pig "is moist, tender and melts in your mouth. When it holds hands with the sauce, they dance!"

All that, plus the crowds of locals who visit at mealtimes definitely make a visit to Deano's worth the short trip into downtown Mocksville.

FROM I-40 Take Exit 170 (US 601/Mocksville). Follow US 601 for 1.5 miles. At a stoplight at the intersection with Wilkesboro St., turn left and go 0.7 mile. Turn left at Gaither and then immediately turn right at North Clement St.

AFTER EATING The Book Rack, home of thousands of used books and two cats, is a couple of blocks away at 114 North Main St.

*Another nearby eatery, Hill's Lexington Barbecue,
is described in the I-73/74 chapter.*

· ·

The Diner

*108 N. Gordon Drive, Winston-Salem, NC 27104 · (336) 765-9158
Monday–Friday 5:30 A.M.–2:00 P.M.; Saturday 5:30 A.M.–12:00 P.M.;
closed Sunday*

According to my Davidson College classmate Dr. Gene Adcock, who introduced me to The Diner, there is good news and bad news. First, the bad news: Steve Eaton Jr., whose grandfather opened the diner in 1968, recently sold the business.

The good news is that the new owners are doing a good job. Gene wrote, "We still go on occasion; many of our former neighborhood friends continue as regulars. Importantly, the food is still good, especially breakfast. The head cook, Poncho, and his family bought the business when Steve decided to retire. They redecorated the place, so that it is much 'fresher' looking but, of course, were smart to keep the food and family-customer ambiance the same. The success of The Diner continues under new management."

The change in ownership made me remember when I fell in love with The Diner on my first visit. "God bless you!" the cashier told a departing customer as I walked in for breakfast one early morning.

My waitress, Stephanie, persuaded me to try the breaded tenderloin with a scrambled eggs plate. It was delicious. When Steve stopped by my table, he explained that, while the breaded tenderloin is a mainstay at The Diner, the most popular item is the black skillet pan gravy, which is served as a separate dish.

Steve told me about his family's long history in the restaurant business in Winston-Salem. His grandfather Raymond Eaton opened The Diner about 1968 in a nearby building. Raymond learned the cooking trade in the navy and then worked at the old

Zinzendorf Hotel in downtown Winston-Salem, leaving that job to open the Main Street Luncheonette, located where the Forsyth County courthouse sits today. With the proceeds from the sale of the luncheonette, Raymond Eaton bought a small existing restaurant with about 9 stools and a counter, paying about $300. Over the years the business expanded. About 1979 Raymond sold the business to his son, Steve's dad. He moved it to its current location and expanded it to about 100 seats. In 1996, his dad sold The Diner to Steve. Just a few months later, Steve's dad passed away. For a long time, Raymond's widow, Rosemary Eaton, came in to make desserts like the banana pudding, cobbler, and pies that are favorites at lunchtime. My waitress, Stephanie Eaton, was Steve's daughter and Rosemary's great-granddaughter.

I asked Steve how this small restaurant could have prospered over four generations of the family. He explained, "There is nothing prim and proper about us. You either like us or you don't. But most people like us. They enjoy picking at me—and I at them. You get to know them by their first names and learn about what is going on in their lives."

"It is sort of like *Cheers*, the old TV program, isn't it?" I asked. "That is about it," Steve replied.

So far the new owners and their families are doing well, but it will take them a long time to catch up with the four generations of Eatons who put their mark on this little *Cheers*-like gathering place.

FROM I-40 At Exit 188 (intersection of I-40, I-40 Business, and US 421) take US 421 West (toward Yadkinville and Wilkesboro). Follow US 421 West for about 0.5 mile. Take the first exit (Exit 239, Jonestown Rd.). At the end of the ramp turn right and head north on Jonestown Rd. Follow Jonestown Rd. for about 0.5 mile until it dead-ends into Country Club Rd. Turn right on Country Club Rd. and go about 1 mile until you reach the intersection of North Gordon Dr. Turn left on North Gordon Dr. and you will see The Diner on the left.

AFTER EATING Walk around the corner to Country Club Rd. and visit Crocodile Used Books, the Train Loft model shop, Reruns thrift store, or the Kit Kringle collectible store.

Little Richard's BBQ

4885 Country Club Road, Winston-Salem, NC 27104 · (336) 769-3457
Monday–Saturday 11:00 A.M.–9:00 P.M.; closed Sunday
www.eatmopig.com

When Gene Adcock told me that the barbecue at Little Richard's was Lexington style and the best in Winston-Salem, I knew I would have to try it out. I was not disappointed.

Richard Berrier, the owner and operator, grew up in Davidson County and learned the art of wood-fired barbecue cooking from Leroy McCarn at the Country Kitchen in Midway. While he was in high school and college, he worked first at curb service, then the cash register, and later in the kitchen, learning every aspect of cooking and providing homelike service. After Richard finished his studies at Appalachian State, Mr. McCarn offered him the chance to run his business, which he did from 1985 until about 1990. In April 1991, after deciding to go out on his own, he opened Little Richard's and has been there ever since.

The inside of Little Richard's takes you back about 60 years, with the jukebox playing songs from the 1950s and '60s. The walls are decorated with old signs that Berrier has collected through the years. He says people bring in old signs for him to display. "That old Coca-Cola clock is probably worth $500 at the flea market," he told me, "but one of my friends brought it here to display, just so other people could see it."

"I'm the only one still cooking with all wood in Winston-Salem," he says. The aroma of the wood cooking adds to the experience. Berrier cooks only the pig's shoulders, making for a clean, delicious, Lexington-style offering. The food is great, but the charm of Little Richard's is its diverse clientele, ranging from judges to ditchdiggers. Berrier says, "The construction workers feel just as comfortable as the judges, because we make them know that they can walk in here with their muddy shoes and feel right at home." And feel right at home I did too, knowing that the next time I'm headed toward the mountains on I-40, Little Richard's will provide an oasis of old-time home cooking just a few miles from the interstate.

FROM I-40 At Exit 188 (intersection of I-40, I-40 Business, and US 421) take US 421 West (toward Yadkinville and Wilkesboro). Follow US 421 West for about 0.5 mile. Take the first exit (Exit 239, Jonestown Rd.). At the end of the ramp, turn right and head north on Jonestown Rd. Follow Jonestown Rd. for about 0.5 mile until it dead-ends into Country Club Rd. Turn left on Country Club Rd., go another 0.5 mile, and you will see Little Richard's on the right.

AFTER EATING Sit in your car for a few minutes and watch the curb service action, which is available from 4:00 P.M. to 9:00 P.M. But be careful. You might be tempted to order something to take with you. Or check out Duke's Restaurant, an inexpensive diner just next door, as a possible place to eat next time.

....

La Botana Home Made Mexican Food

1547 Hanes Mall Boulevard, Winston-Salem, NC 27113
Tuesday–Thursday 11:00 A.M.–9:00 P.M.;
Friday 11:00 A.M.–9:30 P.M.; Saturday 11:00 A.M.–9:00 P.M.;
Sunday 11:00 A.M.–8:00 P.M.; closed Monday

Step inside this busy cantina and you'll be greeted by the delicious smells of real Mexican cooking—their sign even says "Home Made"—but you'll also find friendly faces. Nestled in a small shopping plaza just off Hanes Mall Boulevard, La Botana, which roughly means "snack" in Spanish, might not look like much from the outside, but it's what's inside that counts.

You'll be greeted at the door by a sign announcing "things you should know before you enter." One of those things is they do not serve fancy food or fancy drinks. They're right. They serve good, home-cooked food that is worth the short trip through Winston-Salem traffic to get.

What makes La Botana special? you ask. After all, there are a lot of good Mexican restaurants just a hop and a skip off our state roadways. Well, I'll tell you. The folks at La Botana like to keep you on your toes. They change their menu on a regular basis and feature food you won't usually find in a typical Mexican restaurant, including lamb, asparagus, and tofu. The *Winston-Salem Journal* raves about the *molcajete*, a traditional stew served in a piping-hot stone bowl. Mary Haglund, head chef of Mary's Gourmet Diner in Winston-Salem, loves their authentically cooked beans and veggies. High praise, indeed.

Now, don't get me wrong: you'll also find all the tacos, burritos, and enchiladas you'd expect, all wonderfully prepared. La Botana has been voted best Winston-Salem Mexican restaurant four years running, so they know a thing or two about pleasing people.

But what makes La Botana really special? It's the people. From the family who runs the restaurant to the local customers who religiously gather to enjoy the food, it's the people that make La Botana a true standout and worth finding. Go on a Sunday and you'll see folks from all walks of life in their church clothes, enjoying fried steak *tortas* (Mexican-style sandwiches), quesadillas, and more. Go for lunch or dinner on a weekday and listen to the conversations in English and Spanish, all while soccer matches play on the televisions overhead.

A short trip just off I-40, friendly faces and delicious food await you at La Botana. Just don't fill up on the savory chips and salsa!

FROM I-40 Take Exit 188 from I-40 and merge onto US 421 toward Yadkinville/Wilkesboro. About a mile down the road, take Exit 239 for Jonestown Rd. Take a left onto Jonestown, and in less than a quarter-mile, you will turn left onto Hanes Mall Blvd. La Botana is a quarter-mile down Hanes Mall Blvd. in a small shopping center.

AFTER EATING Hanes Mall is right next door.

Sweet Potatoes

529 Trade Street NW, Winston-Salem, NC 27101
(336) 727-4844, (336) 769-3457
Tuesday–Saturday 11:00 A.M.–3:00 P.M. and 5:00 P.M.–10:00 P.M.;
Sunday 10:30 A.M.–3:00 P.M.; closed Monday
www.sweetpotatoes.ws

In 2003, Stephanie Tyson and Vivián Joiner opened Sweet Potatoes Restaurant in the Downtown Arts District and took the city by storm with their combination of soul food, elegant presentation, and smart marketing. They call their fare "unique, southern inspired" and "uptown, down-home cooking."

Chef Tyson, a North Carolina native, says that she has infused her southern upbringing into the soul of her restaurant. Joiner brings years of restaurant management to the team.

Fried chicken, fried green tomatoes, okra, and other soul food items draw regular customers and visitors from all walks of life. But, even in the historic tobacco town, the sweet potato is king here. The pies, muffins, biscuits, and fries all come from North Carolina's new favorite crop.

Lots of business work gets done here. The *Winston-Salem Journal*'s editorial page editor, John Railey, gives Sweet Potatoes credit for giving him a place to work on his book *Rage to Redemption in the Sterilization Age*.

FROM I-40 Take I-40 Business (Exit 188 or 206). From I-40 Business take Exit 5C for Cherry St. toward the Convention Center. Continue on Cherry St. for about 1 mile. Turn right onto West Fifth St. After 1 block, turn left onto Trade St. Sweet Potatoes will be on the right.

AFTER EATING Walk next door to the corner of Trade and Fifth, where the 100-plus-year-old former U.S. Post Office and Courthouse still stands and has been transformed into the Millennium Center for use for special events. Oprah Winfrey rented the

Sweet Potatoes in Winston-Salem

building to host Maya Angelou's 85th birthday gala. At the party, according to Millennium owner Greg Carlyle, Angelou drank a bottle of Johnnie Walker Blue Label with him.

The Plaza Restaurant

806 NC 66, Kernersville, NC 27284 · (336) 996-7923
Monday–Thursday 11:00 A.M.–8:30 P.M.;
Friday 11:00 A.M.–9:00 P.M.; Saturday 7:00 A.M.–9:00 P.M.;
Sunday 9:30 A.M.–2:00 P.M.
www.plaza-restaurant.com

On my search for the best home cooking places near the interstate, I usually avoid restaurants in shopping centers. I look for family-owned places that have been around a long time. Usually I find them in old, freestanding buildings. These are the places that local people have come to know for their good food and fellowship, rather than for extravagant surroundings designed to attract travelers and other passers-by.

But there are exceptions. So when my friends at the *Kernersville News*, the local newspaper, told me that folks gathered at Plaza Restaurant for good country cooking, I decided to give it a try, even though it sits right in the middle of a shopping center. The restaurant was spiffy clean, and at lunchtime the day I visited, it was completely full. When I tasted my plate of fresh vegetables, I understood why.

When Alex Kroustalis bought Plaza in 1995, he gathered a group of experts to make suggestions about what changes he should make. After due deliberation, they told him, "Change nothing but the lock on the door." Alex followed that suggestion. He attributed his success to four things: "A clean place, good food, reasonable prices, and service. Everything else will take care of itself."

Stephen Kroustalis acquired Plaza from his uncle Alex in 2007. Stephen serves a different set of specials every day, always with a big selection of meats and fresh vegetables. Undoubtedly, one of the secrets to the Plaza Restaurant's success is variety.

Although Stephen has made some extensive changes, including a complete renovation and revamping of the menu, he says he still follows those same old guidelines.

FROM I-40 Take Exit 203 (NC 66/Kernersville). Head north on NC 66 for 2 miles. The Plaza Restaurant is on the left in the Plaza 66 Shopping Center.

AFTER EATING Walk to nearby Granny's Donut Shop and see if you can resist the temptation to eat another dessert.

....

Prissy Polly's Pig Pickin' BBQ

729 NC 66, Kernersville, NC 27284 · (336) 993-5045
Monday–Saturday 11:00 A.M.–8:30 P.M.; closed Sunday
www.prissypollys.com

The judge looked at me with puzzled disdain when he learned that I had omitted this restaurant from an earlier book. "How could you miss Prissy Polly's?" asked Judge Dickson Phillips, former dean of the UNC–Chapel Hill Law School and now retired from the U.S. Court of Appeals. "It's one of our favorite places—some of the best barbecue I have ever had." Lots of people agree, and they sometimes line up outside, knowing they can choose either Lexington- or Eastern-style North Carolina barbecue when they get inside.

When Loran Whaley opened up in 1991 and named his new restaurant after his mother, Pauline, whose nickname was "Prissy Polly," he served Eastern-style barbecue exclusively. But when his sons Greg and Gary noticed that many of their customers were covering their plates with a tomato-based sauce, they determined to add a bit of Lexington to the menu. "It has worked out well for us. And the customers like the option," Greg says.

He emphasizes to me the variety of menu options, including "Cracker Meal Catfish, Low Country Shrimp, Baby Back Spare Ribs, Large Dinner Salads, Fried Chicken, Boneless BBQ Chicken, Chicken Tenders & Brunswick Stew." After taking a breath, he says, "We still offer an array of sides like fried okra, black-eyed peas, barbecued [or grilled] potatoes, country green beans and our now famous loaded potato salad. Desserts include comforting banana pudding, southern pecan pie, key lime pie, apple crisp and chocolate cobbler."

Greg asserts that they are "still serving the best hushpuppies in the state and award winning sweet ice tea." And finally, he brags, "The word has spread far and wide, that heading west of Raleigh-Durham we are the last bastion of Eastern NC style barbecue."

FROM I-40 Take Exit 203 (NC 66/Kernersville). Head north on NC 66 for 2 miles. Prissy Polly's is on the left across from the Plaza 66 Shopping Center.

AFTER EATING Drive to downtown Kernersville to get a look at the famous Körner's Folly, a historic and eccentric three-and-a-half story brick dwelling with a shingled, cross-gable roof located at 413 South Main St.

> *Another nearby eatery, Soprano's, is described in the I-73/74 chapter, and Kepley's Bar-B-Q is also close by. You can find out more about Kepley's in the I-85 chapter.*

. . . .

Stamey's Old Fashioned Barbecue

2206 W. Gate City Boulevard, Greensboro, NC 27403
(336) 299-9888
Monday–Saturday 10:00 A.M.–9:00 P.M.; closed Sunday
www.stameys.com

No list of home cooking spots near I-40 would be complete without a salute to this legendary place.

Three generations of Stameys have made their barbecue business one of the most famous and most successful in the state. Stamey's still holds to its tradition of cooking pork shoulders over wood coals. Even if the barbecue was not so good, I would stop just to order a bowl of their peach cobbler, its flaky, buttery pastry over juicy peaches surrounded by rich, sweet sauce.

But it's the barbecue and side dishes that draw the most people, from Greensboro and all over the state. I saw several teams of construction workers in baseball caps eating at tables next to high-powered women wearing stylish silk scarves. The high ceilings and bright interiors make this restaurant a cheerful place that everybody traveling with you will enjoy.

The founder of the business, Warner Stamey, was born in 1911 and began cooking barbecue when he was in high school. After operating eateries in Lexington, Warner opened his first Greensboro location in 1953. His sons Charles and Keith took over the business and opened the current location in 1979. Keith passed away in 2000. Charles's son, Chip, is the current owner, while Charles, though retired, serves as "pit master emeritus."

Stamey's takes pride in the cooking methods that Warner learned as a boy: "We still slow cook our barbecue over a pit of hardwood hickory coals. The brick pits are completely enclosed, except for a bit of breathing room at the bottom. The hardwood coals are carefully monitored because they will dry the face of the pork if they get too hot. As each 15-pound pork shoulder cooks, the drippings fall onto the hot coals, sending the hickory smoke flavor into the pork."

FROM I-40 Take Exit 217 off I-40. Head north on W. Gate City Blvd. Go about 1 mile (noting the signs directing you to the Coliseum). Stamey's is on the left, directly across W. Gate City Blvd. from the Coliseum.

AFTER EATING Visit the grounds of the massive Greensboro Coliseum just across the street.

Smith Street Diner

438 Battleground Avenue, Greensboro, NC 27401 · (336) 379-8666
Sunday–Monday 6:30 A.M.–2:30 P.M.;
Tuesday–Saturday 6:30 A.M.–9:00 P.M.
www.smithstreetdiner.com

Alton Balance, who lives on Ocracoke Island and is the author of *Ocracokers*, the seminal book about the island, its people, and history, told me that the very best local diner he knew about was Smith Street Diner in downtown Greensboro.

My first thought was that downtown Greensboro might be a little too far away from the big highway to be convenient for travelers. But, I thought, if it's good enough, a trip along Elm St. through old Greensboro and a downtown that is showing great signs of revival might be an added attraction well worth the extra time.

Then I saw a short piece in *Our State* magazine that sang the diner's praises. "Classic diners," wrote David Bailey, "that rely on good food and great service rather than flashy decor and trendy menu items are an endangered species. In this man-eat-biscuit world, Smith Street Diner is a textbook example—a diner that's not only surviving but thriving—and its finest hour is 7:00 A.M. to 8:00 A.M."

By the time I got there about 10:30 A.M. on a Tuesday, the place was still bustling with a breakfast crowd of postal workers in uniform, couples, laborers, and retirees. The waitress told me about one man who comes in three times a day and eats every meal here. I sat down with coffee and looked over the menu and noticed right away their motto: "Open 8 Days a Week."

"So who eats here?" I asked my waitress. "Oh, lots of people," she said. "They come to meet and visit. Right behind you are the UNCG coaching staff. They meet here all the time."

I turned around and pulled my chair up to their booth and said, "Could I have a minute of your time to ask about why you all come here to meet?" "Well, we're having a meeting," one of them told me in a nice but firm way. "So just tell me why you all meet here?"

"Good food, convenient, and nobody bothers us," he said. "Usually, that is."

"Great, thanks," I said. "And can I get your names?" "Mike Roberts," one said. Then, "I'm Wes Miller." And the big guy said, "Jackie Manuel." "Oh my goodness," I said "I've seen you all play for the Tar Heels. I live in Chapel Hill."

I thought to myself, of course Smith Street is like Sutton's in downtown Chapel Hill, the place where basketball players have gathered for generations. And, like Sutton's, Smith Street is a place where a stranger can find friends on the first visit. Owner Beth Kizhnenman is a hands-on manager, and she and her staff are welcoming, especially to newcomers.

FROM I-40 Take Exit 221 for South Elm–Eugene St. toward downtown. Follow South Elm–Eugene St. and Eugene St. for about 3.5 miles to Smith St. Turn right on Smith St. Then immediately turn right onto Battleground Ave. The diner will on the left.

AFTER EATING If you are a Bill Clinton fan, have your photo taken by the plaque that commemorates his visit to the location. Either way, consider a visit to Deep Roots Market, established in 1976, Greensboro's only cooperative, natural goods grocery store, just a block away at 600 N. Eugene St.

Other nearby eateries are described in the I-85 chapter, including Jack's Barbecue, Hursey's Pig Pickin' Bar-B-Q, Angelo's Family Restaurant, Village Diner, and the Hillsborough BBQ Company.

. . . .

Allen & Son

6203 Millhouse Road, Chapel Hill, NC 27516 · (919) 942-7576
Tuesday–Wednesday 10:30 A.M.–4:00 P.M.;
Thursday–Saturday 10:30 A.M.–8:00 P.M.; closed Sunday–Monday

If you pass by Allen & Son, you will be ignoring the advice of Bob Garner, author of *North Carolina Barbecue: Flavored by Time* and other books on our state's foods. Garner says the "homemade, chunky, skins-on" French fries are reason enough to stop.

But he loves the barbecue, too, which is "coarsely chopped into meltingly tender chunks, sprinkled through with shreds of deep brown, chewy outside meat." Not content just to rave about the 'cue and fries, Garner says that Allen & Son serves "one of the tastiest and most authentic versions of Brunswick stew that I've run across."

The man who earned this praise is Keith Allen, who for many years has worked early and late to chop the hickory wood and manage the slow-cooked fire that brings pork shoulders to perfect eating condition. The results of Allen's efforts attract regular visitors from the Chapel Hill–Durham area and faraway visitors traveling I-40 and I-85.

When *Southern Living* named Allen & Son one of its "Top Picks" in southern barbecue joints, they wrote that Keith Allen cooks pork shoulders "Piedmont-style over hickory coals in closed brick pits, but the white mayo-based slaw and spicy, tomato-free vinegar sauce are pure Eastern in nature. North Carolinians from both camps can agree on this, though: the made-from-scratch pies, cobblers, and even the ice cream are the perfect way to finish off the meal."

The Allen family has been cooking and serving barbecue since the 1960s. Most of my friends think that the Allen & Son Bar-B-Que on US 15-501 north of Pittsboro is independently owned, but Keith told me his family is the owner. But, he says, that location "cooks with electricity" rather than the hickory wood coals that Keith gets up in the early morning to get started at the Chapel Hill location.

FROM I-40 Take Exit 266 and head north on NC 86. Go 1.5 miles. Allen & Son is on the left.

AFTER EATING Walk or take a short drive to Lockhart's Trading Post, a combination market, grill, U-Haul dealer, and local gathering place, just in case you didn't meet enough locals at Allen & Son.

Allen & Son in Chapel Hill

. . . .

Margaret's Cantina

1129 Weaver Dairy Road, Chapel Hill, NC 27514 · (919) 942-4745
Monday–Thursday 11:30 A.M.–2:30 P.M. and 5:00 P.M.–9:30 P.M.;
Friday 11:30 A.M.–2:30 P.M. and 5:00 P.M.–10:00 P.M.;
Saturday 5:00 P.M.–10:00 P.M.; Sunday 4:30 P.M.–8:30 P.M.
www.margaretscantina.com

Margaret's began as a Mexican and southwestern-style restaurant.
It still holds to its roots, but over the years, since its founder, Margaret Lundy, emphasized the use of fresh local ingredients, there was a gradual shift toward local cooking styles as well. Among my favorite things about Margaret's are the chips with salsa that arrive at the table almost before you can sit down.

Margaret retired recently and sold the restaurant "recipes and all," but she consults with the new owners to continue the tradition she worked so hard to establish. It has become a local gathering spot for Chapel Hill folks, even though it is a few miles from downtown. Since it is only a minute away from I-40, it gives the traveler an opportunity for a good meal, and for those who love Chapel Hill, it provides a quick and easy way to have a few comfortable minutes with the locals.

FROM I-40 Take Exit 266 and head south on NC 86 (Martin Luther King Jr. Blvd.) toward Chapel Hill. Go 0.5 mile. Turn left on Weaver Dairy Rd. Then turn right into Timberlyne Shopping Center. Margaret's is in the center area of the shopping center.

AFTER EATING Take a walk around the shopping center and check out the eclectic group of stores, including my favorites, the friendly hardware store where I always find something I need, the stationery store, the frozen yogurt shop with tasty desserts, and other tempting places to eat, like the popular vegetarian Sage, as well as Ethiopian, Japanese, Italian, and Mediterranean options.

Other nearby eateries described in the I-85 chapter include Bennett Pointe Grill & Bar, Bullock's Bar-B-Cue, and Saltbox Seafood Joint.

. . . .

Backyard BBQ Pit

5122 NC 55, Durham, NC 27713 · (919) 544-9911
Monday–Saturday 11:00 A.M.–8:00 P.M.; closed Sunday
www.sweetribs.com

I was a big fan of Dillard's Bar-B-Q and Seafood in Durham, where three generations of African American barbecue cooks made a special mustard-flavored barbecue and provided a place for barbecue fans from all walks of life to gather. But Dillard's closed a few years ago, and I needed something like it to take its place in my book. People have been telling me about Backyard BBQ Pit, located on NC 55 going south about a mile from the intersection of NC 54 and NC 55.

When you see Backyard's "rustic" building, maybe you will agree that it is like the unpretentious location in Netflix's *House of*

Cards where Freddie Hayes serves up racks of ribs to South Carolina congressman and soon-to-be-president Francis Underwood, played by Kevin Spacey. Though the two places may look the same, the ribs at Backyard are better than anything you can get in Washington.

I ordered a "working man's" special barbecue sandwich with hushpuppies and baked beans. The hushpuppies counted as one vegetable. I paid $4.99 plus $1.29 for a small glass of iced tea. At the cash register, I asked Michelle Summerville if she could have someone speak with me about the restaurant, and she said, "Of course I will see if Marquis can talk to you." Marquis Egerton II is Michelle's son, and both are part of a large family that operates Backyard in Durham and another restaurant in Roxboro.

"It is a family corporation," Marquis explained to me. He pointed to the other side of the restaurant, where his wife, Brittany, was working. They have two children who are the reason the family is working so hard. "We're taking small salaries and have faith that the hard work we're doing now will build up value for our family." Marquis's uncle Melvin Simmons is the family patriarch and head chef. Sometimes called "Big Paulie," he brought all of his expertise about how to cook barbecue over hickory and oak coals, not to mention his recipes, to the enterprise back in 2007, when this big family took over the former A&W Barbecue location.

The restaurant is not slick. It is just the opposite, deliberately, like an old roadside café from 75 years ago. The walls are covered with magic-marker comments from prior customers attesting to the good food. "We are a barbecue restaurant, but we serve lots of other foods that our customers enjoy. You can call it home style, comfort food, southern food, home cooking or whatever you want to call it," said Marquis, "but we just serve what we think our customers would like to eat."

Though the décor is far from fancy, there is something hanging on their wall that a lot of popular barbecue places lack: a certificate from The Campaign for Real Barbecue attesting that the Backyard meets the standards of the very few barbecue restaurants that cook their barbecue slowly over wood coals.

FROM I-40 Take Exit 278 for NC 55 toward Apex. Follow NC 55 (Apex Hwy.) for about 1 mile. Backyard is on the right.

AFTER EATING Try to persuade Marquis Egerton or Michelle Summerville to show you the small woodburning pit where the barbecue is cooked.

. . . .

Neomonde Raleigh Café/Market

3817 Beryl Road, Raleigh, NC 27607 · (919) 828-1628
Monday–Saturday 10:00 A.M.–9:00 P.M.;
Sunday 10:00 A.M.–7:00 P.M.
www.neomonde.com

When former state legislator Phillip Baddour was chair of the state's Clean Water Management Trust Fund, he asked me to serve as interim director. While we were working closely together, he taught me a lot about the background of his and other North Carolina families with origins in Lebanon. He also persuaded me that North Carolina home cooking should not be confined to barbecue or meat-and-threes when he took me to Neomonde.

In 1977, the four brothers in the Saleh family from Lebanon opened Neomonde as a small baking company. Over time the bakery grew and added a deli, which transformed into a full-fledged restaurant in 2000. The menu is classic Mediterranean, but it is genuine home cooking, so popular in Raleigh that it draws people from downtown and the suburbs to its off-the-beaten-track location near the State Fairgrounds.

FROM I-40 *If headed east:* Take Exit 289 (Wade Ave.). Follow Wade Ave. for 3 miles. Turn right onto I-440/US 1 South. Go 0.6 mile and take Exit 3. At the end of the ramp, turn left on Hillsborough St. Go 0.3 mile and turn right onto Beryl Rd. After crossing the railroad tracks, make an immediate left, and Neomonde is just ahead.

If headed west: Take Exit 293 onto I-440/US 1 North. Go 2.5 miles and take Exit 3. At the end of the ramp, turn right on Hillsborough St. Go 0.3 mile and turn right onto Beryl Rd. After crossing the railroad tracks, make an immediate left, and Neomonde is just ahead.

AFTER EATING The J. C. Raulston Arboretum, a nationally acclaimed garden with one of the largest and most diverse collections of landscape plants adapted for landscape use in the Southeast, is a few blocks away at 4415 Beryl Rd.

· ·

Pam's Farmhouse Restaurant

5111 Western Boulevard, Raleigh, NC 27606 · (919) 859-9990
Monday–Friday 6:00 A.M.–2:00 P.M.; Saturday 6:00 A.M.–12:00 P.M.
MAY NOT ACCEPT CREDIT CARDS

Nancy Olson, the world-famous former owner and bookseller at Quail Ridge Books in Raleigh, told me about Pam's. "It's one of the best country cooking places, ever," she said. "It's got the best red-eye gravy, and there are always interesting people there." When we finally met there for lunch one day, I found out what she was talking about. The southern-style vegetables (collards, okra, and corn) that were offered with my fried chicken were perfectly cooked. I loved the banana pudding and wished that I had had a little more room.

"Pam Medlin has been in the business since she started busing tables at a restaurant that our family owned in Henderson," says Pam's mother, Peggy Robinson. That family tradition continues at Pam's. Her brother, Clay Wade, is a cook and her sister, Tammy Edgerton, is a waitress. Some of the regular customers, who eat breakfast and lunch there every day, are like family, too.

FROM I-40 *If headed east:* Take Exit 289 (Wade Ave.). Follow Wade Ave. for 3 miles. Turn right onto I-440/US 1 South. Go 3 miles and take Exit 2B. See below for directions from Exit 2B. *If headed west:* Take Exit 293 onto I-440/US 1 North. Go 2 miles and take Exit 2B. See below for directions from Exit 2B.

From Exit 2B of I-440: At the end of the ramp, turn left on Western Blvd. Go 0.5 mile. Pam's will be on the left, but the divide prevents a left turn. Go 0.2 mile farther, make a U-turn at the traffic light at Heather Dr. to reverse course, and come back to Pam's.

AFTER EATING Have you ever wanted a sari or wanted to get one for a favorite person? A few doors down at 5107 Western Blvd. is Roopkala Sari Palace, which sells and displays this beautiful clothing.

. . . .

State Farmers Market Restaurant

1240 Farmers Market Drive, Raleigh, NC 27603 · (919) 755-1550
Monday–Saturday 6:00 A.M.–3:00 P.M.; Sunday 8:00 A.M.–3:00 P.M.
www.ncsfmr.com

Although Gypsy Gilliam and her son, Tony, have added some modern dishes to the menu, the State Farmers Market Restaurant is still known for the incredible fresh vegetables, courtesy of the state Farmers Market, the go-to spot for the region's best produce. But there's more to it. These folks also know how to cook it right: squash, greens, collards, beans, corn. And don't forget the biscuits or cornbread, iced tea, and friendly service.

The restaurant also has a museum-quality collection of old-time farm equipment. Civil War memorabilia and North Carolina historical objects line its walls. So even if the food were not so good, this place would be worth a stop. Everybody comes here to eat and meet—businesspeople doing deals, farmers taking a break from selling their crops at the market, working people, and lots of family groups having mini-reunion meals.

If I had one place in the state to take visitors from another country, just to show them what North Carolina was all about, I would bring them right here for the food, of course, but more than that, for the rich diversity and goodness of the North Carolina people who show up to eat here.

FROM I-40 Take Exit 297 (Lake Wheeler Rd./Dorothea Dix/ Farmers Market exit). Head north for 0.25 mile, following the signs to the Farmers Market. The restaurant is the building with the big dome.

AFTER EATING Take a few minutes to walk around the market area. Even if you can resist the extra-fresh vegetables and other crops, you will enjoy the displays and shops. It is a mini–state fair. And if you miss the 3:00 P.M. closing time for the State Farmers Market Restaurant, try the Market Grill or the North Carolina Seafood Restaurant and Market just a few steps away for a late lunch or supper.

Toot-n-Tell Restaurant

903 W. Garner Road, Garner, NC 27529 · (919) 772-2616
Monday–Saturday 5:30 A.M.–8:00 P.M.; Sunday 7:00 A.M.–3:30 P.M.
www.tootntell.co (note ".co" rather than ".com")

If you're anything like me, your first question when you hear the Toot-n-Tell's name is "Where did that crazy name come from?" That question opens the door to more than 60 years of the restaurant's history. Started as a drive-in by Brookie Pool in 1946, Toot-n-Tell served hot dogs, hamburgers, and milkshakes. Customers would toot their horns and tell the carhop what they wanted. After Pool's death, his stepson, Bill Sparkman, and Bill's wife, Maryann, bought the restaurant in 1968. Their daughter, Donna Sparkman Wooten, and Maryann operate the Toot-n-Tell today. Donna has worked at the restaurant for more than 40 years, since she was 13.

Donna, who does not have children, says that she goes to her house to sleep but the restaurant is her home, and the customers and employees are her family. That home is a gift to her visitors, who can find a solid and reasonably priced meal and companionship at any time of the day.

Regular customer Dot DuPree has been eating at Toot-n-Tell "all my life." Her favorite waitress is Lib Mojeske, who is "friendly and smart" and also serves as cashier. Chad Richardson, who works in the area, says the food is like "grandma's cooking, in the day, like the country-style steak and cabbage." He added, "This is the only place I've found that knows how to cook cabbage right." My wife, Harriet, enjoyed the cabbage and turnip greens to go with a fish

Toot-n-Tell Restaurant in Garner

special. Each weekday has a different special with a meat entrée and two vegetables from a long list. Think baked chicken, country-style steak, pork chops, calves liver, and so on. Those who are hungrier or just in a hurry can get a salad bar and a full buffet for less than $8.

Too good to be true. Well, it is not forever. Donna is the end of the family line. But she promises us that she will be there for a long time to come.

FROM I-40 Take Exit 299 for Hammond Rd. and go south on Hammond Rd. for 1 mile to East Tryon Rd. Turn left. Go 0.7 mile and turn right onto Garner Rd. Go 1.7 miles. Toot-n-Tell will be on the right.

AFTER EATING Take a walk in the abandoned graveyard next to the restaurant. The broken gravestones surrounded by weeds and wildflowers can be a reminder of how fragile our monuments can be. Then take a look at the railroad at the top of an embankment right behind the restaurant. The town of Garner grew up around a station of the North Carolina Railroad built in the 1850s between

Goldsboro and Charlotte. Garner is said to have experienced actual combat in the closing days of the Civil War when Sherman's troops were moving along this railroad line toward Raleigh after the Battle of Bentonville.

. . . .

Stephenson's Bar-B-Q

11964 NC 50 North, Willow Spring, NC 27592 · (919) 894-4530
Monday–Saturday 10:00 A.M.–8:00 P.M. (9:00 P.M. in summer);
closed Sunday

This is a favorite eating place for popular mystery writer Margaret Maron, who lives nearby and is a distant cousin of the late Paul Stephenson, who started the restaurant. Paul's son, Andy, who took over a few years before Paul's death, now manages it. Even if you don't see Margaret Maron when you visit, you will surely see some of the models for the characters in her books among the diverse people who frequent the restaurant. When you're eating your chicken and barbecue and slaw, don't forget to leave room for the banana pudding.

I still remember my first visit to Stephenson's with Paul's brother Shelby, later made North Carolina's poet laureate. Paul was still alive and Shelby's wife, Lynda, was in good health. Eating with Shelby and Lynda that night made me determined to find more of these perfect local places to eat and visit.

I couldn't get enough of the slaw—green cabbage, chopped fine, sweet-and-sour flavoring that gave just the right touch to go with the barbecued pork and chicken, Brunswick stew, fried chicken, and hushpuppies. All these were on our table along with big chunks of potatoes covered with a tomato sauce. We were eating and talking like crazy. And when my tea glass got empty, a smiling waitress had it filled before I could think to ask her. When I asked her for some more ice, she grinned and winked and pointed to the bucket that was already on the table.

All of a sudden I remembered some of my friends who travel I-40 to Wilmington, often going back and forth to the beach every weekend in the summertime. I remembered how they sometimes complained that, except for the fast food outlets at the intersections, there is no place on I-40 between Raleigh and Wilmington to stop for a good meal. Oh, if they could only be with us now, I thought. Stephenson's Bar-B-Q is only a mile and a half detour from the interstate. But sadly, only the "insiders" know where it is and how to find it.

Shelby told me about how brother Paul gave up farming back in 1958, developed his own special cooking techniques and sauce, and opened this place for business. That evening, it being Wednesday evening, Paul was at choir practice. "Paul loves to sing," Shelby said, admiringly. "And he will be singing somewhere every Sunday and lots of evenings too." These days you can't help but think Paul is up there, enjoying singing in some heavenly choir.

FROM I-40 Take Exit 319. Head west on NC 210 about 0.5 mile. At the intersection with NC 50, turn right and go 1 mile.

AFTER EATING Stephenson's is probably the only barbecue restaurant in the country that has a commercial nursery next door. Shelby Stephenson says Paul started "messing around" with plants not long after opening the restaurant and pretty soon was selling plants. The business grew and grew. Today the nursery business is strictly wholesale, but that won't keep you from checking it out after your meal.

*Other nearby eateries described in the I-95 chapter include
Broad Street Deli and Market, Sherry's Bakery, Miss
Maude's Cafe, The Diner, and Wilber's Barbecue.*

Meadow Village Restaurant

7400 NC 50, Benson, NC 27504 · (919) 894-5430
Sunday and Wednesday 11:00 A.M.–2:30 P.M.;
Thursday–Saturday 11:00 A.M.–9:00 P.M.; closed Monday–Tuesday
www.meadowrestaurant.biz

Betty Womble from Sanford told me that busloads of folks ride over from Sanford to see the famous Christmas lights in Meadow and then stay to eat at Meadow Village. She raves about the seafood and the homemade desserts. "The chocolate pie is to die for; it's delicious. And there is a really nice salad bar."

Julia Raynor and her husband opened Meadow Village in 1982. Julia still oversees the operation even as she deals with serious injuries stemming from a car accident in 2010. Although paralyzed from the waist down, she still moves about the restaurant in a motorized wheelchair, bringing optimism and cheer to her customers. Julia and her son, Timmy, are proud of their low prices: about $8 for the lunch buffet and about $12 for the huge spreads in the evening and on Sunday at noontime.

Becky Lupton, who has worked at Meadow for 20 years, 5 years as manager, cheerfully greets guests at the door and collects advance payments for the bountiful buffet that awaits them.

"Don't miss putting Meadow in your book" is advice I got from countless friends for whom Meadow is a special treat on the way to the beach. Don't you miss it, either.

FROM I-40 Take Exit 334 and follow NC 96 toward Meadow for 0.7 mile. Turn left onto NC 50 and go about 100 yards.

AFTER EATING During the Christmas season, the lights in this tiny town attract visitors from all over eastern North Carolina. The Bentonville Battlefield is about 15-20 minutes away, well worth a visit if you have never seen it.

Meadow Village Restaurant near Benson

· ·

The Country Squire

748 NC 24 Business, Warsaw, NC 28398 · (910) 296-1727
Sunday-Friday 11:30 A.M.–2:00 P.M. and 5:30 P.M.–9:30 P.M.;
Saturday 5:30 P.M.–9:30 P.M.
www.countrysquireinn.com

Maybe the Country Squire is a little too "upscale" to fit in the
"home cooking" category. But so what if it is a little fancy; it is
still a gathering place for folks from all over Duplin County. My
friend Tom Kenan says he makes it a point to stop by for a meal
whenever he visits Liberty Hall, the old Kenan family homeplace,
now restored and open to visitors. Owner Iris Lennon, a native of
Scotland, has given her restaurant, inn, and surroundings a festive
European touch.

FROM I-40 Take Exit 364 and follow NC 24 Business (College St.)
for about 3 miles, passing through Warsaw. Turn right onto NC
24-50 Business. Go 4 miles. Country Squire and Vintage Inn will be
on the left.

AFTER EATING Visit the gift shop or ask Iris to give you a tour of her winemaking operation and consider buying a bottle to remember your visit.

....

Holland's Shelter Creek Fish Camp

8315 NC 53 East, Burgaw, NC 28425 · (910) 259-5743
Wednesday–Sunday 11:00 A.M.–8:00 P.M.
(open to 9:00 P.M. on Friday and Saturday); closed Monday–Tuesday

Very few old-time fish camps are left anymore in North Carolina. One of them is Holland's Shelter Creek Fish Camp, and it is a very convenient 6 miles from I-40. In the early 1980s, while Steve Holland was driving around looking for land to buy for a campsite, he stopped at a store for directions. He wound up buying the store and turning it into a restaurant. He has added on and rebuilt, adding boat rentals, campsites, and fishing supplies. But the main attraction is the food with generous servings of scallops, catfish, shrimp, and oysters. And if you want to try frog legs, they fry them up for you.

Retired Presbyterian minister John Goodman says he welcomes the chance to preach occasionally at various churches, more so when his route home takes him near Holland's and he can stop for the "delicious food and generous portions" at Sunday lunch. Holland's was something of a secret pleasure for a group of regular visitors until it was featured in the *Raleigh News and Observer*'s "Best Kept Secrets" series in 2015.

FROM I-40 Take Exit 398 for NC 53 East toward Jacksonville. Go 6 miles. Holland's will be on the right.

AFTER EATING Find a seat overlooking Shelter Creek, which flows into the Northeast Cape Fear River, and watch the water go by. Visit Holland's general store, which stocks local food products like Apple Pie Moonshine jelly. Barnyard Antiques and Flea Market across the road is full of potential treasures. Consider renting a canoe and exploring the creek like Ann and Bland Simpson did in their book *Little Rivers and Waterway Tales: A Carolinian's Eastern Streams*. Or drive about 5 miles to the site of the former Carolina Industrial School, also described in the Simpsons' book, located at 3747 Croomsbridge Rd., about 4 miles away via NC 53 and Croomsbridge Rd.

· ·

Paul's Place Famous Hot Dogs

11725 US 117, Rocky Point, NC 28457 · (910) 675-2345
Open every day, 6:00 A.M.–10:00 P.M.
(11:00 P.M. on Friday and Saturday)

Paul's Place is not exactly a home-style restaurant, but the hot dogs are legendary. My friend Ben Barker (father of the famous former chef at Durham's Magnolia Grill) says it is a "must" stop. "These dogs are different. Go all the way with onions and slaw and his special sauce—not chili!"

Stewart McLeod, who works at the newspaper in Clayton, told me, "You can't leave out Paul's Dogs. . . . It's the best hot dog I've ever eaten. Once, while in college at UNCW, I ate five for lunch. Today, if I am in the area, I stop even if it's not lunch time."

According to McLeod, the unique red relish at Paul's is "a holdover from the World War II era when beef was rationed. Since your standard chili was not then an option, Paul's came up with its famous relish recipe."

Today Paul's Place is "where the local men hang out to swap stories at lunch time," a Castle Hayne resident told me. David Wilson Paul, the third-generation owner of Paul's, agreed: "I'll talk your ear off." His grandfather started Paul's in 1928. "Back then, they were open 24 hours a day. When my granddad died back in 1939, they had to nail the doors shut to close the place so they could go to the funeral. Before that, they never had any need for locks. It was always open."

Paul's still stays open most of the time. But it closes for a few hours at night. And Paul's has made one other concession to

Paul's Place Famous Hot Dogs in Rocky Point

modern pressures: It now serves chili. "We didn't want to, but so many people asked for it, we just went ahead and added it."

David Jonathan Paul, the fourth generation of his family, took my order recently. He says nice things about all the state's college football and basketball teams, but if you mention N.C. State, his alma mater, he breaks into a wide smile. Paul's also serves a full breakfast and has other items on its menu. But most people still stop just to get one of those famous hot dogs.

FROM I-40 *If headed east:* Take Exit 408. Turn left on NC 210. Go 0.3 mile to US 117. Turn left and go 3.5 miles. Paul's is on the right.

If headed west: Take Exit 414. Head west on Holly Shelter Rd. toward Castle Hayne. Go about 1 mile into Castle Hayne. At the intersection of Holly Shelter Rd. and NC 117, turn right (north) onto NC 117. Follow NC 117 going north for about 3 miles. Paul's is on the left.

AFTER EATING On weekends, a busy flea and farmers market sets up next door. It is a great place to meet local people.

Casey's Buffet

5559 Oleander Drive, Wilmington, NC 28403 · (910) 798-2913
Wednesday–Saturday 11:00 A.M.–9:00 P.M.;
Sunday 11:00 A.M.–8:00 P.M.; closed Monday–Tuesday
www.caseysbuffet.com

I first heard about Casey's from my friend Bob Woodruff, who stopped me one day at the grocery and said, "Hey, I've got the place for you. While we were at the beach last weekend, we were driving down Oleander in Wilmington and I saw the Casey's sign with the pig on it. That is usually a good omen."

He told me there was an all-you-can-eat buffet and that the restaurant was full of all kinds of people, mostly working folks. He said that the tab was $11.99 ($10.99 for seniors) with a buffet full of fried chicken, baked chicken, barbecue, whiting fish, and chitterlings. Every day, he exclaimed, they had pigs' feet. I told Bob it sounded like soul food, and he said it was. He liked the okra even though it wasn't fried. He did say there was one problem: "I got full before I was ready to stop eating!" Still, Bob found room to get a sample of two kinds of fruit cobbler before he left. It sounded too good to be true, but I found that Bob Woodruff had only scratched the surface of the good things to eat at Casey's.

I did a little research and found that Casey's is a nationally known soul food restaurant. One fan raved that it is "the real deal" and "a soul food-lover's dream come true. . . . They have pretty much everything: fried chicken, chitterlings, fatback, chops, okra . . . you name it. Unlike many buffets, everything is fresh, hot, and scratch-made."

Larry Casey and his wife, Gena, opened the restaurant about 10 years ago. Previously, Larry had spent about 10 years at the Wilmington branch of Taste of Country before it closed.

Casey's has a slogan: "Miss ya Mama's cookin' . . . Come home to Casey's."

My wife, Harriet, and I loved everything on the buffet line, just as Bob Woodruff said. We could not believe how crisp and delicious the fried catfish tasted. Larry explained that he has a special source from a farm near Greenville.

"When UNC-TV's Bob Garner visited us," Larry told me, smiling, "he liked the catfish, too. And he mentioned our source in Ayden. All of a sudden, they couldn't supply us anymore because they had sold out to people who heard about it from Bob. But we've gotten that straightened out and they are taking care of us again." Larry told me that the best-selling vegetable is "okra, pan fried, unbreaded and lightly seasoned, which I fashion after my grandmother Kitty Casey."

Something else was very special for us. Even though Casey's was crowded with folks coming from church on that Sunday, people on the staff, including Larry and Gena, were extra friendly and helpful to every customer.

FROM I-40 Where it turns into North College Rd. (US 117), follow North College Rd. for 4 miles to Oleander Dr. Turn left and go 2 miles. Casey's is on the left.

AFTER EATING Now that you are in Wilmington, there is no limit to the "must visit" places to see. For instance, Airlie Gardens, with its 67 acres of historical gardens, is only about 2.5 miles away via Oleander Dr. and Airlie Rd. The nearby campus of UNC-Wilmington is lovely and worth a drive through. Even closer, in fact right across the street at 5570 Oleander Dr., you can take a few minutes to watch the hitting practice at Stadium Batting Cages.

INTERSTATES 73 & 74

"Why don't you find us some home-cooking places near our new interstates I-73 and I-74?" Folks began to ask me this question a few years ago when the future I-73 and I-74 signs began to appear on some of our highways.

At first, I resisted. It is tough enough to cover the locally owned, family-operated restaurants that are near enough to the "real" interstates to give an alternative to the fast food franchises that surround the intersections.

Then I looked at the proposed routes and saw that there would be some good gathering places to eat near the proposed routes—places like the Snappy Lunch in Mount Airy near I-74, made famous by Andy Griffith.

So let's give it a try. And if you are willing to go a little way off the interstate, you will find there is good eating at some nice friendly places along the way.

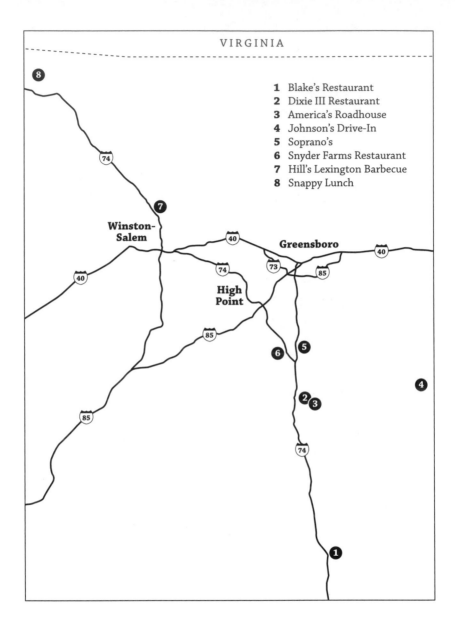

VIRGINIA

1 Blake's Restaurant
2 Dixie III Restaurant
3 America's Roadhouse
4 Johnson's Drive-In
5 Soprano's
6 Snyder Farms Restaurant
7 Hill's Lexington Barbecue
8 Snappy Lunch

Winston-Salem

Greensboro

High Point

Blake's Restaurant

127 Hillview Street, Candor, NC 27229 · (910) 974-7503
Monday–Friday 6:00 A.M.–8:00 P.M.;
Saturday–Sunday 7:00 A.M.–2:00 P.M.

In 1947, after Colon Blake came back from army service in France during World War II, he opened Blake's Restaurant. At first, he bought an old truck stop, fixed it up, and opened up shop. Then, in about 1955, he built a new structure on old US 220 near Candor and Biscoe. The restaurant became a community gathering place and one of the best places to stop on that north-south route that runs right through the middle of North Carolina.

About 1985, when US 220 Bypass was built around Candor, Blake saw the handwriting on the wall. So he had his building moved 2 miles to its current location, where the bypass (now the new interstate) intersects with NC 211. I remember when I visited him a few years ago, Blake encouraged me to order the chicken pot pie, saying I ought not to pass it up, but I selected another one of the specials. My fried chicken, butter beans, corn, and mashed potatoes were mighty good, and after I finished my special plate, Blake told me to try the coconut cream pie. When I said I was full, he said, "No, you have to try it. I'm going to pay for your dessert." That was a hard offer to resist. Made on the premises, it is as good a dessert as I can ever remember having.

When Blake became seriously ill in 2007 and died soon afterward, his staff and family rallied to show that, thanks to his mentoring, they would be able to keep his restaurant going strong, even if he were no longer there every minute to check on things.

FROM I-73/74 Take the NC 211/Candor exit. Head west on NC 211 toward Candor for a few hundred feet, then turn right into the Blake's Restaurant parking lot.

AFTER EATING In summer, visit one of the many fine peach orchards and stands near Candor. About 10 minutes south of Blake's is Johnson's Farm at 1348 Tabernacle Church Rd., Candor. It is open most of the year even when peaches are not available. Ken Chappell Peaches & Apples, Kalawi Farms, and other fine orchards are 5 or 10 minutes away on NC 211 going east toward Eagle Springs and are open seasonally from mid-June.

....

Dixie III Restaurant

715 East Dixie Drive, Asheboro, NC 27203 · (336) 625-8345
Monday–Friday 11:00 A.M.–9:00 P.M.; closed Saturday–Sunday

Asheboro attorney Ricky Cox makes his way to Dixie III at least three times a week because "their fried shrimp is so good." His friend Alan Pugh says Ricky is crazy to pass by all the other special plates that Dixie III offers—"meat and three vegetables or spaghetti." Mark Davidson started the Dixie III when he was 25 years old, having grown up working with his dad, former county commissioner Kenyon Davidson, who started the original Dixie Restaurant in Asheboro more than 50 years ago. Now Mark's son, John, is helping his dad run the restaurant. This Asheboro restaurant family takes pride in "full service—meats, seafood, homemade desserts, plus fresh vegetables in season like pinto beans, fried okra, squash, green beans. We've got customers from every walk of life—suit, ties or mud on your shoes, it's all okay with us."

Mark told me Pat McCrory made a campaign stop here in 2012. My good friend the late Keith Crisco, a rare Asheboro Democrat who served as the state's secretary of commerce, told *Business North Carolina* that Dixie III's "food is great and that's where business gets done. I take everybody there."

FROM I-73/74 Take the Asheboro/US 64 exit. Head east on US 64 toward Siler City and Raleigh. Go 2 miles. Dixie III is on the left.

AFTER EATING You are only about 10 minutes away from the North Carolina Zoo via NC 159, now called the Zoo Parkway. Drive downtown to the Collector's Antique Mall. If you have less time and are more adventurous, consider a quick visit to Treasure World Gun & Pawn just down the street.

. . . .

America's Roadhouse

818 East Dixie Drive, Asheboro, NC 27203 · (336) 633-1234
Tuesday–Thursday 11:00 A.M.–9:00 P.M.;
Friday–Saturday 11:00 A.M.–10:00 P.M.;
Sunday 11:00 A.M.–9:00 P.M.; closed Monday
www.americasroadhouse.com

My college classmate Bob Auman of Raleigh told me that he happened to find America's Roadhouse "by luck and by chance" while traveling through Asheboro and that he thoroughly enjoyed the oysters and the Hawaiian chicken salad.

On a recent visit Bob ordered the fried oysters. "One of the co-owners/co-managers said that fresh seafood from Louisiana is trucked in regularly. The oysters were super, and the serving was more than ample."

When I stopped by on a late Friday morning, it was almost full, mostly with seniors. But, said co-owner Joe Robertson, a different mix was going to keep them busy all weekend long. Joe and his partner, Andy Archibald, opened their business in 2002, after working together for other restaurants. "We thought we could do a better job on our own."

"What is your secret?" I asked. "Fresh seafood," he said. "We pile it high."

They also offer a "zoo menu" in honor of the nearby North Carolina Zoo, serving up ostrich, buffalo, alligator, and frog legs.

FROM I-73/74 Take the Asheboro/US 64 exit. Head east on US 64 toward Siler City and Raleigh. Go about 2 miles. America's Roadhouse is on the right after you pass Dixie III on the left.

AFTER EATING Check the "After Eating" suggestions for nearby Dixie III.

Johnson's Drive-In

1520 East Eleventh Street, Siler City, NC 27344
Note: no telephone and no drive-in service
Tuesday–Saturday 10:00 A.M.–2:00 P.M.; closed Sunday–Monday
MAY NOT ACCEPT CREDIT CARDS

Johnson's Drive-In is a long way from I-73/74 and, in fact, a bit far from any interstate. But it's worth the trip. For years, every time I saw him, Randy Gardner told me, "You mean you live so close, and you've never been to Johnson's? Their cheeseburger is the best in the world."

Then there were other legends about Johnson's that I wanted to check out. "Get there early. When he runs out, he closes. And it can be well before 2:00 P.M."

People explained that Johnson's owner estimates the amount of ground beef he needs for each day, grinds it fresh each morning, and when he runs out, that's it. There are no more cheeseburgers that day.

Other people told me that it was not the ground beef. He would shut down each day when he ran out of buns.

Former North Carolina House of Representatives speaker Joe Hackney backed up what everybody else said about Johnson's, adding, "You know, the owner, Claxton Johnson, is my cousin. And another cousin, Wade Hackney, eats there every day, same time each day, like clockwork. Get there early because Claxton really does run out—every now and then. Even if he doesn't run out, it gets mighty crowded at lunchtime, and you might not be able to find a seat."

"So," I asked Joe, "what is the secret of this special cheeseburger?"

"Well, one of these secrets is the big thick block of 'cheese' Claxton pushes down on top of the burger," Joe said. "And you know what it really is? It's Velveeta."

Having heard so much about Johnson's, I was ready when longtime friend Jamie May invited me to eat lunch with him there. When we arrived about 11:30, it was already crowded. But we found

Johnson's Drive-In in Siler City

seats at the counter. From there we watched Claxton presiding over the grill, making each burger individually on order.

"They taste different, you know, depending on what you put on the bun. A lettuce and tomato cheeseburger is an entirely different thing from one with chili and onions," Claxton told us. But the quick hint of a smile told me he thought his burgers were the best, whatever else he put on them.

"So what is the real secret to your cheeseburgers?" I asked.

"Mainly, it's the beef—midwestern, grain fed—ground fresh every day and put on the grill only when I get the order. And, everything that's not used on one day, meat, slaw, chili, or anything else, gets tossed out. I am not going to ruin that good beef with day-old slaw."

FROM I-73/74 Take the Asheboro/US 64 exit. Head east on US 64 toward Siler City and Raleigh. Go about 23 miles. Johnson's is on the south side of US 64 (Eleventh St.) where it intersects with East Raleigh St.

AFTER EATING Consider experiencing the rich Latino culture in Siler City with a visit to Tienda Loma Bonita, a store and café at 214 Martin Luther King Jr. Blvd., not far from Johnson's, for a selection of imported food products. The Loma Bonita name comes from a town in Mexico in the Oaxaca area, the hometown of the owners who now live in Siler City. If you are still hungry, try an authentic Mexican dish at the café in the back of the store.

· ·

Soprano's

638 West Academy Street, Randleman, NC 27317 · (336) 498-4138
Daily 10:30 A.M.–10:00 P.M. (11:00 P.M. on Friday and Saturday)

The man responsible for Soprano's and its reputation for solidly good Italian dishes is not Italian at all. Ossama Hashish hails from the Mediterranean region, Alexandria, Egypt, but he has been in North Carolina for some time. He managed a restaurant in Asheboro for about five years before opening Soprano's in 2000. You don't have to sing for your supper, but you might sing Soprano's praises after a meal. The Italian food is great, and lots of customers order the lunchtime meat-and-two-vegetables special. Randleman is the original home of the famous auto-racing Petty family, and they still live close by, regularly ordering takeout from Soprano's.

FROM I-73 Take Exit 82 (Academy St./Randleman). Head east on West Academy St. for about 0.5 mile, passing through a roundabout. Soprano's is on the left at the far end of a strip shopping center.

AFTER EATING The Petty Museum at 309 Branson Mill Rd., Randleman (Level Cross), is about 10 minutes away via I-73 headed north. Four generations of the Petty NASCAR racing family, Lee, Richard, Maurice, Kyle, and Adam are featured. Folks at Soprano's also suggest a visit to Sweetie's Frozen Yogurt at 991 High Point St., in the Walmart Shopping Center.

Snyder Farms Restaurant

2880 Beckerdite Road, Sophia, NC 27350
(336) 498-3571 or, for catering, (336) 498-4872
Thursday–Saturday 5:00 P.M.–9:00 P.M.;
Sunday 11:30 A.M.–2:00 P.M.; closed Monday–Wednesday

This NASCAR-themed restaurant is a veritable temple to Richard Petty. When Petty's mother visited a few years ago, she exclaimed to her son, "Richard, they have more of your junk in here than you do at home!"

But it's the food that keeps locals coming back for supper on Thursday, Friday, and Saturday and lunch on Sunday. What food! Fried chicken, country ham, country-style steak, fried fish, hushpuppies, corn, slaw, and fried green squash. And homemade yeast rolls, biscuits, and banana pudding.

Betty and Wayne Snyder have been serving the Randleman area since 1984, offering homemade fried chicken, fried squash, banana pudding, and other southern favorites. Their children, David and Annette, are helping continue the tradition.

Hal Powell, a frequent visitor, says "Snyder's is probably the best buffet in the state! I surely think so!"

FROM I-74 (ALSO US 311 BYPASS) Take Exit 84 and turn right onto US 311. Go 0.5 mile and turn left onto Beckerdite Rd. Follow Beckerdite Rd. for 2 miles.

AFTER EATING Hang around the restaurant to be sure you have seen all the important Richard Petty memorabilia.

Other nearby eateries described in the I-40 chapter include The Diner, Little Richard's BBQ, Sweet Potatoes, The Plaza Restaurant, Prissy Polly's Pig Pickin' BBQ, Stamey's Old Fashioned Burbecue, and Smith Street Diner. You'll find Tommy's Bar-B-Que, Captain Tom's Seafood Restaurant,

Pioneer Family Restaurant and Steakhouse, Mary B's Southern Kitchen, and Kepley's Bar-B-Q in the I-85 chapter.

· ·

Hill's Lexington Barbecue

4005 North Patterson, Winston-Salem, NC 27105 · (336) 767-2184
Tuesday–Sunday 7:00 A.M.–8:00 P.M.; closed Monday

Hill's has the qualities I look for in a North Carolina eatery. It is a community gathering place where good food draws lots of local customers. Join in as the crowds gather at breakfast for bountiful offerings of pancakes and scrambled eggs. The barbecue is cooked over wood coals and counts barbecue experts like Jim Early as fans. It features a homemade signature dish, warmed banana pudding topped with meringue. It is convenient, just off the future I-74 interstate.

One more thing: Hill's has been around since 1951, when Joe Allen Hill and his wife, Edna, opened their restaurant. Joe Hill came from Lexington and put his hometown in the name to identify the style of barbecue he planned to offer. Some barbecue historians say that Hill's was the first to put Lexington in its name.

FROM I-74 (US 52) Take Exit 113 for Patterson Ave. Go north on Patterson Ave. for about 1 mile. Hill's will be on the right.

AFTER EATING Visit Bethabara Park at 2147 Bethabara Rd. (less than 10 minutes away via Motor Rd. and Indiana Ave.). This 1753 historical site of the first Moravian settlement in North Carolina sits within a wildlife preserve and has a reconstructed village and church. "Grounds, gardens, and trails open free of charge, all day, all year." Call ahead at (336) 924-8191.

Another nearby eatery, Lantern Restaurant, is described in the I-77 chapter.

Snappy Lunch

125 North Main Street, Mount Airy, NC 27030 · (336) 786-4931
Monday–Saturday 6:30 A.M.–1:30 P.M. (1:15 P.M. on Saturday);
closed Sunday
www.thesnappylunch.com

When I travel in other countries, I try to connect the people I meet to North Carolina by describing something they already know and then explaining the connection. I try things like tobacco and cigarettes, the Wright Brothers' first flight, Michael Jordan, Billy Graham, Bank of America, the Research Triangle Park, and so on. Lately, I have been thinking about mentioning former Davidson College basketball player Stephen Curry. Sometimes, but not often, one of these connective links works, but there is one that almost always does: Andy Griffith and Mayberry. "So you come from where Andy lived," they say. And I then have a new friend.

Maybe, then, a trip to Mayberry or Mount Airy, where Andy really grew up, should be on every North Carolinian's bucket list. A trip there would not be complete without a visit to Snappy Lunch, where Mount Airy residents—like the real Andy and many others—have eaten since it opened in 1923. "Make it snappy," some customers said when they ordered a sandwich. Hence the name, Snappy Lunch.

Longtime owner Charles Dowell created Snappy Lunch's classic, a pork chop sandwich described as "a boneless, tenderized loin chop dipped in sweet-milk batter and fried until golden crisp."

Although Dowell died in 2012 at age 84, his legacy still is felt. His widow, Mary, and daughter, Jamie, own and operate Snappy Lunch with help from Jamie's husband, Seth Dowell-Young, who is in charge of the grill, where Charlie used to hold court. The family is determined to keep Charlie's legacy alive. Mary's great-nephew, Brady Horton, took my order for the famous pork chop sandwich, all the way. He brought it to me wrapped in wax paper, almost dripping with juicy slaw, tomato, and sauce, with pork so large it was poking outside the bun.

The fare is simple and good, mostly sandwiches at lunch. Breakfast is served until 10:30 a.m. Raymond Keith Massey was eating breakfast while I ate my sandwich. He told me he came "five times a week." When I asked why so often, he said, "It's cheap, two eggs and a big piece of pork, just $2.14."

Massey then told me that he really came for the fellowship. He admires Mary for taking care of others. "If you ain't go no money, you can eat for free. Mary just says to them, 'Somebody else has already paid for you.'"

Remember: Do not leave without sampling that pork chop sandwich. It's worth the trip.

Author Lynn York grew up in nearby Pilot Mountain. In her debut novel, *The Piano Teacher*, she wrote about a small-town restaurant called the Squeezebox. Its real name was the Luncheonette, but it was crowded at lunch, hence the nickname. Because she writes about "a grill full of sizzling pork chops and fried baloney," could Snappy Lunch have made its way into her novel, renamed as the Squeezebox?

FROM I-74 Take Exit 11 onto Rockford St. toward Mount Airy. Go 3 miles to Graves St. (on the left). Turn left onto Graves St. Follow Graves St. (which become Dixie St.) for 0.2 mile to Franklin St. Turn right and follow Franklin St. for 0.1 mile. Turn right on North Main St. (a one-way street) and go 0.1 mile. Snappy Lunch will be on the right.

AFTER EATING Walk up and down Main St. Visit the City Barber Shop and ask who cut Andy's hair. At 301 North Main is the Mount Airy Museum of Regional History, and a few blocks away at 218 Rockford St. is the Andy Griffith Museum. Both museums charge a reasonable admission fee.

INTERSTATE 77

"Isn't it about time that you came home, D. G.?" I was glad to get this question. It is always nice when someone from your hometown says they wish you would move back.

"Oh, no," she said, "I meant that you should write about some of the good home cooking places to eat around here—next time you do one of your interstate eating books."

Maybe she was right. I traveled all across North Carolina on the interstates trying to find good home-style places to eat near the intersections. Not the fancy, new places, but the old restaurants, cafés, and local gathering places. I tried to find places where the locals eat and where visitors are made to feel at home.

But I neglected I-77, the road that runs right through the town where I grew up, the city where I practiced law for 20 years, and the place my wife and I raised our children. These are places where my North Mecklenburg High School football teammates Tommy and Donnie Ohler and their dad, J. W., first introduced me to their great barbecue, now famous thanks to the annual Mallard Creek Barbecue. Finally, as a result of two close but unsuccessful campaigns for the U.S. Congress, I learned more about the fellowship and friendship-building at local eateries than I did about winning elections.

So my friend was right. I should not neglect the places where my love of fellowship and food had arisen.

Following my friend's suggestion, I gathered a few of my old favorite places along I-77 and some new ones to share with you.

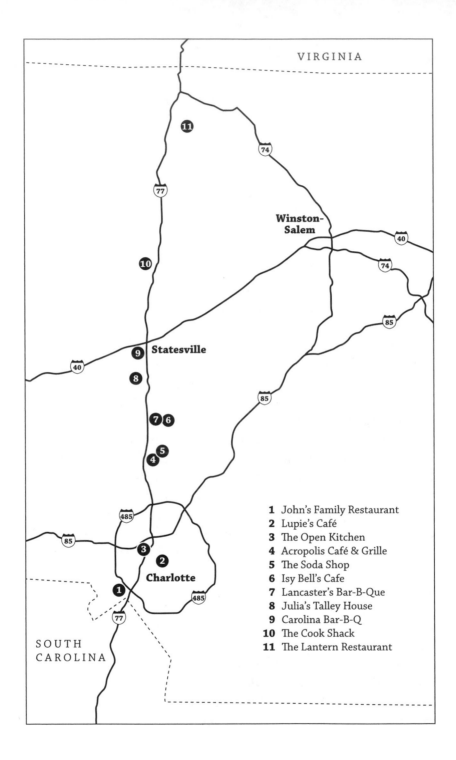

1 John's Family Restaurant
2 Lupie's Café
3 The Open Kitchen
4 Acropolis Café & Grille
5 The Soda Shop
6 Isy Bell's Cafe
7 Lancaster's Bar-B-Que
8 Julia's Talley House
9 Carolina Bar-B-Q
10 The Cook Shack
11 The Lantern Restaurant

Maybe this chapter will help you find a pleasant place to stop and eat. If it does, then we can both be glad that I did go home again.

I-77 takes us from the crowded urban areas where Charlotte spills over into South Carolina all the way to the sparsely populated mountain border with Virginia. Along the way, I will guide you to a couple of genuine home cooking restaurants in the Charlotte area, take you to a sandwich shop in my hometown, give you an option to eat family-style in a historic house, sit you down where Charles Kuralt critiqued the barbecue, show you where local old-time music and food come together, and give you a chance to eat in a small county seat community.

· ·

John's Family Restaurant

2002 Westinghouse Boulevard, Charlotte, NC 28273 · (704) 588-6613
Monday–Saturday 11:00 A.M.–9:00 P.M.; closed Sunday

If you visit John's Family Restaurant on Wednesday nights, you will join folks who are stopping by after church choir practice to get a plate of southern home-style vegetables. The owner, John Tsoulos, makes a promise on the menu: "No Canned Vegetables." Or at lunchtime you can stand in line with crowds of folks who work in the industries and offices that line Westinghouse Boulevard and the nearby areas of southern Mecklenburg County.

John specializes in local, southern-style food. But it didn't come naturally. He grew up in Greece, left school and went to work at age 10, got a job on a cruise ship, jumped ship in New York in 1970, and made his way to North Carolina.

"It's all right to talk about it now. I have been legal for a long time. And everybody knows I love America," John told me when I stopped by to sample his food.

John's customers love him, too. They admire the way he is always working. "You would never know he is the owner from the way he cleans off tables, checks the orders, and backs up his crew wherever he is needed."

John's Family Restaurant has been open at this location for about 15 years. Earlier he occupied the building across the street where another restaurant is now located. The "new" home is bright, clean, very comfortable, and big enough to seat up to 250 people—almost enough to take care of the lunchtime crowd.

I learned about John from former state senator Fountain Odom, who lived nearby for many years and says that John is one of America's great success stories. And I learned from John that he loves to talk to his customers about his love of hard work, fresh southern-style vegetables, and, most of all, his love for America.

FROM I-77 Take Exit 1 (Westinghouse Blvd.). From the intersection, head west on Westinghouse Blvd. (If you are headed south, it will be a right turn off the long exit ramp; if you are going north, turn left.) Go about 1.5 miles. John's Family Restaurant is on the right, at the intersection with Pioneer Drive.

Another nearby eatery, United House of Prayer for
All People, is described in the I-85 chapter.

. . . .

Lupie's Cafe

2718 Monroe Road, Charlotte, NC 28205 · (704) 374-1232
Monday–Friday: 11:00 A.M.–10:00 P.M.;
Saturday: 12:00 P.M.–10:00 P.M.

Guadalupe (Lupie) Durand learned how to cook simple foods from Lillie Mae White, the cook at the old Thompson Orphanage in Charlotte. Lupie went to live at Thompson Orphanage when she was 13. "She pretty much cooked everything from scratch," Lupie remembers of Lillie Mae. Since Lupie's opened in 1987, its simple, homemade, inexpensive dishes have drawn a diverse and loyal set of fans. "I started making chicken and dumplings because it was cheap. But people like things plain and simple."

Lupie's may be best known for its chilies. It has three different ones: Texas, Cincinnati, and vegetarian. But the honest food and surroundings, Lupie's welcoming spirit, and the diverse and friendly folks who fill up the restaurant have always made meal-time a happy time for me.

FROM I-77 *If headed north:* Take Exit 9 (US 74 East/I-277 North/ John Belk Fwy.). Follow I-277 for 2 miles. Take Exit 2B onto US 74 East (Independence Blvd.) Follow Independence Blvd. for 2 miles. Turn right onto Briar Creek Rd. Go 0.5 mile. Turn right onto Monroe Rd. Go 0.5 mile. Lupie's is on the left.

If headed south: Take Exit 11 (for I-277 South/Brookshire Fwy. East/NC 16 South). Merge left onto I-277 South. Go 1.8 miles. Bear left to take Exit 2B (US 74 East/East Independence Blvd.). Follow Independence Blvd. for 2 miles. Turn right onto Briar Creek Rd. Go 0.5 mile. Turn right onto Monroe Rd. Go 0.5 mile. Lupie's is on the left.

AFTER EATING Just a few blocks away at 2700 East Independence Blvd. is the Bojangles Coliseum or the "Old Charlotte Coliseum." When it opened in 1955, it was the largest unsupported steel dome in the world. Still looking like a giant spaceship, it is worth a drive-by.

. . . .

The Open Kitchen

1318 West Morehead Street, Charlotte, NC 28208 · (704) 375-7449
Monday–Thursday 11:00 A.M.–11:00 P.M.;
Friday-Saturday 11:00 A.M.–11:30 P.M.; Sunday 4:00 P.M.–10:00 P.M.
www.worldfamousopenkitchen.com

Even from a distance of miles and time, whenever I remember my visits to the Open Kitchen as a teenager, I think about the red-checked table cloths, the brick walls, the old political buttons, post-cards, celebrity photos, and college pennants on display—each one put up individually over a long period of time. And I remember how special the Open Kitchen was when I was in high school and college.

The food was good, filling, and reasonably priced. And the folks who ran the place and those who worked for them were friendly.

It is still pretty much the same today. And it is therefore, for me, a welcome place to go back in time.

New Year's Eve in 1959 was one of the low points of my life. Our Davidson basketball team was struggling. We had been clobbered by Wake Forest and Tennessee. Our coach had lined up a "pushover" game for us against Erskine. Because the college was closed for the holidays, we played the game in a small gym in Mooresville. Underdog Erskine trounced us. It was so bad that the coach even let me play at the end of the game.

Humiliated, we made our way to the Open Kitchen to try to "celebrate" the New Year. As soon as we arrived, we ran into "Big Bill" Ward, the WBTV sports anchor, and he told us we ought to cheer up, because "you all are going to be great—someday." That helped. What helped more was a group of telephone operators who had worked the evening shift and had come to the Open Kitchen for their New Year's Eve party. When they learned that we were basketball players, they treated us like heroes rather than losers. "We are Southern Belles," they laughed. And we laughed, too. And Davidson basketball has been on the upswing ever since. Awash in all these personal memories, I thought of something that is important to you. The Open Kitchen is just a few blocks off the interstate. And no hungry, lonely traveler should pass it by.

Stephanie Kokenes is the fourth generation of her family to work in the restaurant business in Charlotte. Her father, Alex, manages the Open Kitchen. Her grandfather Steve and his brother opened the restaurant in 1951. And her great-grandfather Constantine ran the Star Lunch in downtown Charlotte beginning in the early 1900s.

All that tradition comes together at today's Open Kitchen, which got its name because Steve Kokenes wanted his customers to feel free to look inside the kitchen to see how the food was being prepared. That tradition still holds. Longtime employee Sue Brandon, who served our group cheerfully, is another tradition. When I asked why she'd stayed at Open Kitchen so many years, she told me, "It is just a good place to work—it's like home."

The food is home style too, Italian home style, even though the Kokeneses originally came from Greece. Sue Brandon told me that the lasagna is the most popular dish among the "regulars." But John Malatras, who has worked with the family for many years, says that their pizza is still a big favorite. "You know, they introduced pizza to Charlotte back in 1952. And people would come from all over just to try it out. It is still good!"

FROM I-77 *If headed north:* Take Exit 9 and then Exit 9C, following signs to US 74 West for 0.2 mile, and take Exit 1A to merge onto Freedom Dr. Go about 0.5 mile and turn right onto West Morehead St. Open Kitchen is on the left. (Note that getting back on the interstate going north is real easy. Ask for directions at the Open Kitchen.)

If headed south: Take Exit 10A (Morehead St.). At the end of the ramp, turn right onto West Morehead St. Follow West Morehead St. for about 3 blocks. The Open Kitchen is on the right. Just before you get there, you will see a big, colorful sign that says "Alte! The Open Kitchen." The restaurant and its parking lot are just a few doors away. (To get back on the interstate going south, ask for directions at the Open Kitchen.)

. . . .

Acropolis Cafe & Grille

20659 Catawba Avenue, Cornelius, NC 28031 · (704) 894-0191
Monday–Friday 7:00 A.M.–10:00 P.M.;
Saturday-Sunday 8:00 A.M.–10:00 P.M.
www.acropoliscg.com

I know this place well, because it is where my North Mecklenburg class of 1958 meets for a Saturday lunch every few months. It's a big place, and lots of other groups meet here regularly. In fact, when U.S. Senator Thom Tillis was a member of the Cornelius Town Board, he came every first Thursday at 8:30 A.M. to have breakfast and talk business with his fellow board members.

The "Southenders," a group of retirees, mostly newcomers to the area, meets every month for breakfast. About 80 members gather to talk business and build friendships and connections.

My North Mecklenburg High group likes the good solid food options and the pleasant service. Judy Hefner told me, "We chose the Acropolis because the staff has treated us royally for our 42 quarterly luncheons since we began in 2004." She says "the Davidson Chicken Salad is popular, but everyone selects from the great variety of good foods there from hamburgers to spaghetti, etc. The food is always just right. Helen has been our server forever, always with efficiency and a bright smile. It is a warm and friendly place and so accommodating."

Another classmate, Barbara Ledford, told me her favorite dish is the white garlic pizza, which was one of the popular recipes of Acropolis's Pete (Panagiotis) Dimitri Kapakos, the patriarch of the family that owns the restaurant. Pete died in 2014 at 93. He was born in Sparta, Greece, immigrating to the United States when he was in his mid-20s. Prior to coming to North Carolina, he owned New Canaan Pizza in Connecticut. His daughter, Joanne Kapakos Teis, and son and daughter-in-law, James and Christine Kapakos, are the current owners and managers of the Acropolis.

FROM I-77 *If headed north:* Take Exit 28 and merge onto US 21 South/Catawba Ave. Go 0.3 mile and turn left onto Holiday Ln. Acropolis will be on the right.

If headed south: Take Exit 28 toward US 21 North/Catawba Ave. Keep left at the fork, follow signs for US 21, and merge onto US 21 North/Catawba Ave. Go 0.5 mile and turn left onto Holiday Ln. Acropolis will be on the right.

AFTER EATING Visit the Cornelius branch of the Charlotte Mecklenburg Library, a few blocks away at 21105 Catawba Ave., and ask to see materials and exhibits about the history of Cornelius.

The Soda Shop

104 South Main Street, Davidson, NC 28036 · (704) 896-7743
Monday–Thursday 10:00 A.M.–2:00 P.M.;
Friday–Sunday 8:00 A.M.–2:00 P.M.
www.davidsonsodashop.com

The Soda Shop owner Deborah Caudle explained her restaurant's special charm to me like this: "If you crave nostalgia or want to drift back to your college days or childhood, this is the place. The walls may not talk, but they tell a story of the history of the restaurant and customers."

You might think I am suggesting The Soda Shop just to get you to stop in my hometown of Davidson. While it's true that I want to share that wonderful place with all my friends, The Soda Shop would be well worth a stop, even if it weren't right in the middle of one of the nicest towns in the world.

You know you're in a college town when you walk in the door and see pennants and sports photos on the walls. For me the experience is extra special because The Soda Shop is almost exactly like the M&M Soda Shop that served Davidson students and townspeople while I was growing up. And when I order orangeade and an egg salad sandwich, it is a miracle. They are just as good as when Murray Fleming and Mary Potts made them for me more than a half-century ago. They cost a little more today, but they are still worth every penny.

The refreshing fruit drinks, the sandwiches, and the ice cream make The Soda Shop special, especially since Deborah has expanded the offerings to include a wide variety of dishes. But what I like best is that you can stop at any booth and folks will treat you like a long-lost friend.

FROM I-77 Take Exit 30. From the intersection, head east on Griffith St. toward Davidson. Go about 1.5 miles, until you reach a dead-end at the Davidson College campus about a block after you cross the railroad tracks. Turn right on North Main St. Go about 2

The Soda Shop in Davidson

long blocks. The Soda Shop is on the right in the center of David-son's small business district.

AFTER EATING Take a walk down the friendliest Main Street you will find anywhere. If you have an extra few minutes, take a short walk across the Davidson College campus. I bet you will start to understand why I am so glad that "I can go home again." But be careful. If you stay in Davidson much longer, you won't want to leave.

Isy Bell's Cafe

1043 North Main Street, Mooresville, NC 28115 · (704) 663-6723
Monday–Saturday 6:00 A.M.–9:00 P.M.;
Sunday 7:00 A.M.–2:00 P.M.

The first thing I noticed about Isy Bell's Cafe was the sign on the outside. It said in big bold letters "HOME COOKING," and I knew I had come to the right place. Isy Bell's is near Mooresville's downtown, which is more than just a little way from the interstate intersections.

With all the development near the interstates, even some of the old Mooresville residents have forgotten about their local restaurant treasures. Thank goodness for Phil Alexander at the Iredell County Solid Waste Disposal Facility, who finally told me, "D. G., if you want real home cooking, then there's no question but that you have got to go all the way into town and try Isy Bell's. That is where they all go."

So off I went, winding myself away from I-77, around the northern edge of Mooresville, and then into the downtown area along North Main Street. A little bit outside the main business center I found my "home cooking" sign and knew I had come to the right place.

I opted for the special plate with four vegetables and iced tea. I got mashed potatoes with great beef gravy, cabbage, corn, a combination of okra and tomatoes—and a biscuit and cornbread. Perfect!

After I finished my great vegetables, I looked around the room and saw an old friend, Presley Brawley. Presley had campaigned for me when I was a political candidate many years ago. "D. G., I tried," he said, "but you came in here and told the dairy farmers that they needed to help clean up the streams that ran alongside their pastures. And you told all my hunting friends that they had to get involved in the gun safety movement. All that did not sell too well up here. We liked you, and we tried to help all we could. But you didn't make it easy."

I laughed, but I did have to ask Presley how he could just jump me with all of his complaints so many years after the campaign had ended—almost before he told me hello.

"Well," he said, "I'm now the senior member of the Iredell County bar, and I can say just about whatever I want, whenever I want—and I do." We had a good laugh about that.

Presley wasn't reticent about talking about the food at Isy Bell's Cafe either. He and his law partner, Brian Harwell, come here regularly to discuss business, meet their clients, and enjoy the good food.

"Take the selection of vegetables first," Presley said. "They have 20 different vegetables listed, and they will all be fresh. If you come in the morning you'll be surrounded by contractors. They get in here and meet and get their work lined up and make deals with each other. It is like a contractors' hall."

He then told me, in no uncertain terms, not to forget about the desserts. He was right about that. The peach cobbler had a wonderful breadlike crust that complemented the sweet, fresh peaches inside. Pressley told me that the strawberry cobbler is even better. But Isy Bell's owner, Mike Kabouris, had to give me the bad news. He had just run out of that dish. I guess it just gives me one more reason to go back to Isy Bell's—as if I needed another reason.

FROM I-77 Take Exit 36 (Mooresville/NC 150). From the intersection, head east on NC 150 toward Mooresville. Go through a very developed area for about 3.5 miles until you reach the intersection of NC 150 and NC 801 (West Park Ave.). Turn right on West Park Ave. and follow it for about 1 mile until it intersects with North Main St. (also NC 152). Turn left and go about 0.5 mile, passing a Food Lion store just before you reach Isy Bell's Cafe, on the right.

AFTER EATING Make your way to 215 North Main St. to see the Charles Mack Citizen Center, said to be "Mooresville's premier event venue." It honors the father of John Mack, former head of Morgan Stanley, who gave $4.5 million to expand the center. Charles Mack's father, also named John, came from Lebanon in 1903. He came to Mooresville by accident when a railroad agent in New York put him on the wrong train. He peddled clothing for a living, and one of the rooms in the Citizen Center is named the "Peddler Room" in his honor.

. . . .

Lancaster's Bar-B-Que

515 Rinehardt Road, Mooresville, NC 28115 · (704) 663-5807
Monday–Tuesday 11:00 A.M.–9:30 P.M.;
Wednesday–Saturday 11:00 A.M.–10:00 P.M.
www.Lancastersbbq.com

Lancaster's proudly serves Eastern-style barbecue right in the middle of Lexington-style barbecue territory. The barbecue is mighty fine, but the special reason to visit is a chance to celebrate Mooresville's close connections to the stock-car racing industry. The restaurant is decorated with racers' uniforms, flags, photos, and full-size racing cars. Lancaster's even has a full-size school bus on the floor, with tables inside for those who want to eat there. Lots of locals eat here, along with plenty of the famous racecar drivers.

FROM I-77 Take Exit 36. Head east on NC 150. Go 2 miles, crossing US 21, to NC 152. Immediately turn left onto Rinehardt Rd.

AFTER EATING Don't leave Lancaster's without inspecting all the displays and decorations that celebrate the local connection to stock cars and their drivers.

Julia's Talley House

305 North Main Street, Troutman, NC 28166 · (704) 528-6962
Monday–Friday 11:00 A.M.–2:00 P.M. and 5:00 P.M.–8:30 P.M.;
Saturday 5:00 P.M.–8:30 P.M.; Sunday 11:00 A.M.–2:00 P.M.
www.juliastalleyhouse.com

"It is like Sunday dinner, but Grandma doesn't have to cook," Eric Wilkinson of Mooresville told me as he and his wife, Jennifer, waved goodbye to his parents, grandmothers, a great-great aunt, and another carload of relatives heading back to Lincolnton after a family meal at Julia's Talley House in Troutman.

"It is just a great place for us to come from different places and meet," Eric continued. "And my great-great aunt says the food is even better than it used to be." Julia's has been around since 1979, when Julia Shumate first opened her restaurant in the former home and office of a beloved family doctor. In fact, Dr. Talley had delivered Julia. So she honored his memory by putting Talley in her restaurant's name.

Approaching the entrance, I walked up to Dr. Talley's front porch. The rocking chairs were full of folks who had finished their meals and just wanted to visit a little longer. Just inside the house is a big portrait of Julia, who, until she died a few years ago, checked on things at the restaurant nearly every day.

Julia Shumate is gone, but her restaurant is still owned and operated by Shumate family members, Kim, Joe, and Chris, who currently manage the day-to-day operations.

Inside, Julia's is still more like a house than a restaurant. And Eric Wilkinson was right. I got a family-style meal that was served just like an old-time Sunday dinner. They served me 10 different bowls of food, family-style, even though I was eating alone. If I had not been so hungry, I could have gone to the cafeteria line, paid a little less, and eaten more modestly. But I will choose family-style at Julia's every time. At suppertime and for the noontime meal on Sundays, Julia's fills up with families, both locals and people coming from miles around. At weekday lunchtime, things move a little fast, and Julia's provides a bargain meat-and-vegetable plate that includes iced tea. What to eat at Julia's? Fried chicken is its specialty, and it was great. But the country ham made the meal. The vegetables are better in the summer when more of them are fresh, but the plentiful selection will always give lots of good choices.

FROM I-77 *If headed north:* Take Exit 42 (US 21/Troutman). At the end of the ramp, turn left and head north toward Troutman on US 21 and NC 115. Go for about 3 miles to Troutman. Just beyond the small downtown of Troutman you will see Julia's Talley House on the left.

If headed south: Take Exit 45 (Troutman). Follow the signs to Troutman. Here is what you will do: At the end of the ramp, turn right onto Amity Hill Rd. Then after a few hundred yards, turn left onto Murdock Rd. Follow Murdock Rd. for about 2 miles until it dead-ends into US 21/NC 115. Turn left (south) on US 21/NC 115 toward Troutman. Just before you reach Troutman's downtown, you will see Julia's Talley House on the right.

Other nearby eateries, including Sunshine's Café and Keaton's BBQ, are described in the I-40 chapter.

Carolina Bar-B-Q

213 Salisbury Road, Statesville, NC 28677 · (704) 873-5585
Monday–Thursday 10:30 A.M.–8:00 P.M.;
Friday-Saturday 10:30 A.M.–9:00 P.M.

Gene and Linda Medlin have been cooking pork shoulders over hickory wood coals here since about 1985. "Charles Kuralt stopped by and ate our barbecue," Gene says, "and you know what he thought about [it]?" Without waiting for an answer, he says, "Not much. Said there wasn't enough fat and gristle in it."

The Medlins have taken Kuralt's criticism to heart, but they haven't changed their "refined" way of cooking. Instead, they've posted a handwritten note on the cover of *Charles Kuralt's America* displayed prominently beside the cash register: "Extra fat and gristle available on request."

Actually Kuralt was most complimentary, writing that the Medlins "cook their barbecue over a hickory fire all night, at least twelve hours, which is right; and they baste it with a mild vinegar sauce they call 'kitchen dip,' which is right." Then he complained, "But they cook only whole pork shoulders, which is wrong. It results in a barbecue which is too refined, without the necessary grease and gristle." For those of us who like pork shoulders, the Medlins have the perfect product. Others should just request the extra fat and gristle.

Linda is proud of their hushpuppies. In a *Statesville Landmark and Record* article about Carolina's thirtieth anniversary, she said, "They're crunchy on the outside and soft on the inside."

In addition to the barbecue-related menu items, they serve up seafood, chicken, salads, and country vegetables.

FROM I-77 Take Exit 49B (Statesville/Salisbury Rd.). Turn right onto Salisbury Rd. Continue toward downtown for 1.5 miles. Carolina Bar-B-Q is on the right.

AFTER EATING Take about a 3-block walk to the Statesville Civic Center at 300 South Center St., where you can view renowned North Carolina artist and Statesville native Ben Long's fresco titled *Images at the Crossroads*. It features Hecate, a Greek goddess associated with crossroads, appropriate because Statesville is the crossroads of I-77 and I-40. But Hecate is also associated with magic and witchcraft. This created an interesting controversy when the fresco was first displayed. Nearby, take a look at the old city hall, constructed around 1890. North Carolina architecture expert Catherine Bishir writes that architect Willoughby Edbrooke's building embodies "Romanesque monumentality at its most handsome and restrained."

The Cook Shack

1895 West Memorial Drive, Union Grove, NC 28689 · (704) 539-4353
Monday–Friday 8:00 A.M.–6:00 P.M.; Saturday 8:00 A.M.–4:00 P.M.
MAY NOT ACCEPT CREDIT CARDS

On Saturday mornings at The Cook Shack, owners Myles and Pal Ireland host a jam session with dozens of fiddlers and banjo and guitar pickers. It's a gathering that has been called "the oldest continuous bluegrass jam session in the world."

If you can't make the jam sessions on Saturdays, though, try out the great cheeseburgers through late lunchtime any weekday. Pal cooks a great breakfast, and on cool days she'll serve warm soup or plates of pintos and cornbread. Because Myles and Pal have a small grocery store at The Cook Shack, you can find local folks to keep you company at almost any hour of the day.

FROM I-77 Take Exit 65 (NC 901/Union Grove). Follow NC 901 for 1.5 miles toward Union Grove. The Cook Shack is on the left just past the fire station.

AFTER EATING Enjoy browsing the store's walls and shelves crowded with bluegrass and country music memorabilia. Visit Union Grove General Store at 1932 West Memorial Hwy. Walk the grounds of "The Ole Time Fiddler's & Bluegrass Festival" at 1819 West Memorial Hwy.

Another nearby eatery, Snappy Lunch,
is described in the I-73/74 chapter.

The Lantern Restaurant

304 North Main Street, Dobson, NC 27017 · (336) 356-8461
Monday–Saturday 5:00 A.M.–9:00 P.M.; closed Sunday

Mount Airy and Elkin may be the biggest cities in Surry County, but little Dobson is the county seat. At mealtime, the center of social life in Dobson is The Lantern, where Clinton and Maxine Dockery have served breakfast and country-cooking meat-and-vegetable plates in the same location since 1972. Actually, the restaurant burned down once. Clinton Dockery built it back, telling me that The Lantern is "pretty much the same, because I liked it like it was."

In 2010, the Dockerys sold The Lantern to Betty Foster, and, sadly, a few months later, Clinton Dockery died. With the help of her manager, Ruth Kidd, and longtime Lantern employees Louise Houston and Rodney Dockery, Foster now carries on Clintons and Maxine's tradition serving the courthouse crowd and locals their favorite home-cooked vegetables, fried chicken, meats, oysters, pulled pork sandwiches, and a changing array of meat-and-two-vegetable special plates, reasonably priced at $5.99.

FROM I-77 Take Exit 93 (Dobson). Head east toward Dobson for about 3 miles. At the second stoplight, turn left on Main St., and The Lantern will be on the right.

AFTER EATING Dobson is surrounded by some of North Carolina's finest wineries. But if time is limited, you can still enjoy a quick visit to the downtown and old courthouse.

INTERSTATE 85

I-85 just might be North Carolina's main street. It joins our state's major urban areas, and because its intersections are so crowded by development, the search for old-time home cooking places can be frustrating. Still, there are many opportunities to sit down with local people along the way. You can sample barbecue not only in Lexington but also in Gastonia, Rowan County, High Point, Hillsborough, Durham, Butner, Henderson, and Norlina. If barbecue is not your thing, I will take you to a variety of other places to mingle with the locals and eat home-style cooking.

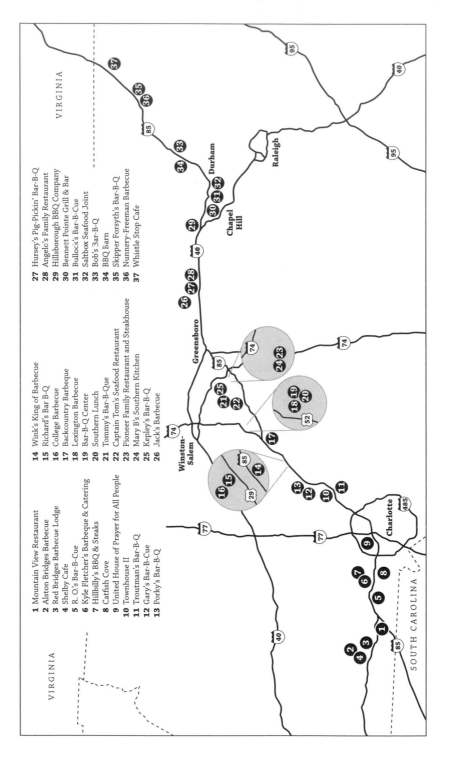

VIRGINIA

VIRGINIA

1 Mountain View Restaurant
2 Alston Bridges Barbecue
3 Red Bridges Barbecue Lodge
4 Shelby Cafe
5 R. O.'s Bar-B-Cue
6 Kyle Fletcher's Barbeque & Catering
7 Hillbilly's BBQ & Steaks
8 Catfish Cove
9 United House of Prayer for All People
10 Townhouse II
11 Troutman's Bar-B-Q
12 Gary's Bar-B-Cue
13 Porky's Bar-B-Q

14 Wink's King of Barbecue
15 Richard's Bar B-Q
16 College Barbecue
17 Backcountry Barbeque
18 Lexington Barbecue
19 Bar-B-Q Center
20 Southern Lunch
21 Tommy's Bar-B-Que
22 Captain Tom's Seafood Restaurant
23 Pioneer Family Restaurant and Steakhouse
24 Mary B's Southern Kitchen
25 Kepley's Bar-B-Q
26 Jack's Barbecue

27 Hursey's Pig-Pickin' Bar-B-Q
28 Angelo's Family Restaurant
29 Hillsborough BBQ Company
30 Bennett Pointe Grill & Bar
31 Bullock's Bar-B-Cue
32 Saltbox Seafood Joint
33 Bob's Bar-B-Q
34 BBQ Barn
35 Skipper Forsyth's Bar-B-Q
36 Nunnery-Freeman Barbecue
37 Whistle Stop Cafe

SOUTH CAROLINA

Mountain View Restaurant

100 West King Street, Kings Mountain, NC 28012 · (704) 734-1265
Monday–Saturday 6:30 A.M.–9:00 P.M.; Sunday 11:00 A.M.–4:00 P.M.

If you are traveling back and forth to South Carolina, Mountain View is a good place to say "hello" or "goodbye" to small-town North Carolina. In the winter, you can get a good view of Kings Mountain, where the patriots won an important battle in the American Revolution. Although Mountain View is a relatively new restaurant, the owner, Nick Mantis, former head cook at the Athens Restaurant in Charlotte, and his daughter, Georgia, the manager, have earned a loyal local clientele for their country cooking, lunch specials, and tasty Greek dishes. The law office of North Carolina Speaker of the House Tim Moore is nearby, and he is a regular for breakfast.

FROM I-85 *If headed north:* Take Exit 8 and follow NC 161 toward Kings Mountain for 1.5 miles. Turn left at E. King St. and go 0.5 mile.

   If headed south: Take Exit 10B and follow US 74 West for 1.5 miles. Exit onto E. King St./US 74 Business West and follow E. King St. for 1.5 miles.

AFTER EATING Assuming that you don't have time to visit the Kings Mountain Battlefield Park, walk a few blocks to the Kings Mountain Historical Museum at 100 East Mountain St. It is open Tuesday–Friday until 4:00 P.M. Free admission.

Alston Bridges Barbecue

620 Grover Street, Shelby, NC 28150 · (704) 482-1998
Monday–Thursday 10:45 A.M.–10:00 P.M.;
Friday–Saturday 10:45 A.M.–8:30 P.M.; closed Sunday

Shelby tourist officials promote the rivalry between two cherished local barbecue joints, Alston Bridges Barbecue and Red Bridges Barbecue Lodge. "Award winning BBQ and part of the unspoken BBQ war in Cleveland County," they say. "With two Bridges Barbecue restaurants you will have to decide which is your favorite."

Some refuse to decide. Ron Rash, famous author of the best-selling novel *Serena* grew up nearby. When asked about his favorite place to eat, he says simply, "Bridges Barbecue in Shelby."

The two Bridges families are not blood kin, but they are bound together heritage-wise. Barbecue expert Jim Early says both Alston Bridges and Red Bridges learned their craft of cooking pork shoulders over hickory coals from the legendary Warner Stamey, the godfather of Lexington-style barbecue (which some people say should be called Shelby-style barbecue). Alston was Stamey's brother-in-law. As Warner Stamey's grandson Chip Stamey explained in John and Dale Reed's *Holy Smoke*, "All us barbecue guys are inbred."

Alston's grandson Reid Bridges and Red's granddaughter Natalie Ramsey agree that each has a loyal set of customers and there is plenty of business to keep both families busy.

So, which is better, Alston's or Red's? Locally, both have their loyal followers. Some are so loyal that they have never eaten at the "other Bridges." But consider visiting both and making your own decision. I've eaten at both places, and I am going back several more times before I make up my mind.

FROM I-85 Take Exit 10B and follow US 74 West about 15 miles to Shelby to the intersection of US 74 and NC 18 (South LaFayette St.) Turn north toward Shelby and follow NC 18 (LaFayette St.) for 2 miles to the intersection with East Grover St. Turn right to follow

NC 18 and East Grover St. Go 0.7 mile. Alston Bridges is on the right.

AFTER EATING Visit downtown Shelby. See the entry for Shelby Café, below.

· ·

Red Bridges Barbecue Lodge

2000 East Dixon Boulevard, Shelby, NC 28150 · (704) 482-8567
Wednesday–Sunday 11:00 A.M.–8:00 P.M.; closed Monday–Tuesday

About 10 years ago, on my first visit to Red Bridges's one day a little after noon, I sat at a counter and ordered a barbecue sandwich and sweet tea. Both were delicious. While I was eating, an older lady, dressed as if she were going to church, came in alone. She smiled and greeted the wait staff, and soon one of them brought her a plate with two hotdogs. She held up her hand to protest, saying, "You all know my doctor told me not to order hotdogs anymore."

"But Mama B., you didn't order them," the server said. "We just brought them to you."

"Well, if I didn't order them," she said, as she took a bite of the hotdog, "it will be okay to eat them, wouldn't it?"

I figured out that Mama B. was Lyttle Bridges, the widow of Red Bridges, and that this little drama played out regularly at the noon hour.

Lyttle and Red opened their first barbecue restaurant in 1946. When Red died in 1966, Lyttle ran the business until she retired at 80 years old. Red and Lyttle's daughter, Debbie Bridges-Webb, runs the business with help from her children, Natalie Ramsey and Chase Webb.

Jim Early, author of *The Best Tar Heel Barbecue: Manteo to Murphy*, saved his highest praise for Red: "The woodsy, smoky, nutty-flavored pork is tender to a fault and, with sauce, is THE BEST. . . . The tangy brownish-red sauce is tart with sweetness. The sweet and sour makes your tongue and taste buds tango and your soul happy. I love this stuff."

In the spring of 2015, *Garden & Gun* conducted a best-barbe-cue-in-the-South voter poll, patterned on the NCAA basketball tournament's "Sweet Sixteen." Red Bridges triumphed, winning the top spot. "Although based in a North Carolina town of less than 30,000," the editors said, "the sixty-six-year-old barbecue joint, known for its chopped pork shoulder, hushpuppies, and vine-gar-sauced red coleslaw, managed to rally its fan base and come out on top of all five rounds." One taste and it's easy to see why.

FROM I-85 Take Exit 10B and follow US 74 West about 15 miles to Shelby to Red Bridges Barbecue Lodge at 2000 East Dixon Blvd. (US 74). The Lodge is on the left. You will pass it and make a U-turn to reach it.

AFTER EATING Visit downtown Shelby. See the entry for Shelby Café, below.

· ·

Shelby Cafe

220 South Lafayette Street, Shelby, NC 28150 · (704) 487-8461
Monday–Saturday 6:00 A.M.–8:30 P.M.;
Sunday 6:00 A.M.–3:00 P.M.

There are plenty of reasons to visit Shelby Cafe. Locals connect here, breakfast is available all day, and solid meat-and-vegetable plates are served at lunch and supper. But livermush, a combination of various parts of the pig flavored with spices, is my main reason for leading you here. Thanks to North Carolina food guru Bob Garner's book *Foods That Make You Say Mmm-mmm*, I learned the cooks at Shelby Cafe "will prepare your livermush pretty much to order, and they'll serve it inside a fluffy biscuit, next to fried eggs and grits, worked into a livermush and cheese omelet, or muddled into a breakfast casserole with eggs, cheese, mushroom soup, and sautéed onions."

Shelby businessman David Royster introduced me to cafe own-ers George Rizkallah and Bryan Greene, who served me a plate of crispy, juicy livermush so good that I wake up at night wanting to taste it again.

Livermush is a popular local food in the western Piedmont and one of those things you have to eat to be a "real North Carolinian." The Shelby Cafe makes this initiation rite a pleasant one.

FROM I-85 Take Exit 10B and follow US 74 West about 15 miles to Shelby to the intersection of US 74 and NC 18 (South LaFayette St.) Turn north toward Shelby and follow NC 18 (LaFayette St.) for 0.7 mile. Shelby Cafe is on the left facing West Arey St.

AFTER EATING Visit the museum at the Earl Scruggs Center in the old courthouse building at 103 South Lafayette St., which "combines the life story of legendary five-string banjo master and Cleveland County native, Earl Scruggs, with the unique and engaging story of the history and cultural traditions of the region in which Mr. Scruggs was born and raised."

. . . .

R. O.'s Bar-B-Cue

1318 West Gaston Avenue, Gastonia, NC 28052 (704) 866-8143
Monday–Saturday 10:30 A.M.–9:00 P.M.; closed Sunday
www.rosbbq.com

Gastonia native Stephen Bryant told me about this restaurant, which has been a part of Gastonia for more than a half-century. Stephen told me how his parents had courted there when you could get two "slaw burgers" and a Coke for 32 cents. His parents went back recently, and as they pulled up beside the restaurant, a carhop came out to serve them just the way they did so many years ago, when Stephen was no more than just a gleam in his parents' eyes.

The special today, if you can believe it, is still the slaw burger. The slaw burger is a sandwich filled with slaw. But what slaw! Juicy with just the right amount of mayonnaise, it surprises with added tomatoes and some secret spices that give it a wonderful flavor. But you ought to try the barbecue and slaw combination for a real treat.

Robert O. Black, the R. O. in the restaurant's name, opened up shop in 1946. His son, Lloyd, ran the place for many years with the help of Mark Hoffman, Lloyd's nephew and R. O.'s grandson. Mark has taken the lead now, but Lloyd drops by regularly. Either can tell you about Gastonia history.

Has R. O.'s changed much since 1946?

"Throughout the years, we have modified our style none," Lloyd says. "People grew up eating here and now their children eat here and work here."

If you miss the old-time experience of the drive-in restaurant, do like Stephen's parents. Wait outside and let the carhops come to you.

FROM I-85 Take Exit 17 (Gastonia/US 321 South). Head south on US 321 (North Chester St.) and go 1 mile to Airline Ave. Turn right and go 1 mile. (Airline becomes West Gaston Ave.)

AFTER EATING Less than a mile away at 300 South Firestone St., at the corner of West Second Ave., is Loray Mill, the site of a 1929 labor strike. The historic textile mill has been preserved and converted to a mixed-use community.

. . . .

Kyle Fletcher's Barbeque & Catering

4507 Wilkinson Boulevard, Gastonia, NC 28052 · (704) 824-1956
Tuesday–Saturday 11:00 A.M.–8:00 P.M.
MAY NOT ACCEPT CREDIT CARDS

Kyle Fletcher says he got his start cooking when a friend needed barbecue for a wedding reception. Then he leased the building that formerly housed Bland's Barbecue and revamped it for his "charcoal and hickory" method of smoking. I've heard some people just drive by to enjoy the smells that come from his old-time cooking. Weighing in on the "Eastern vs. Lexington" controversy, Kyle says, "I don't put nuthin' on my meat—except hickory and charcoal smoke. That way they've got an option to put whatever sauce they want on my barbecue." Lots of local people agree with Kyle, and sometimes you'll find them lined up to enjoy the generous and reasonably price wood-flavored servings. Kyle brags about his restaurant's recognition as the "Best of Gaston" by the *Gastonia Gazette*.

FROM I-85 Take Exit 22 toward Cramerton/Lowell. Turn left onto South Main St. Go 0.3 mile and turn left onto Wilkinson Blvd. Go 0.4 mile. Kyle's is on the left. You will have to make a U-turn at Westover St. to reach it.

AFTER EATING Across the street at 4520 Wilkinson Blvd. is All Things Collectible. It is jammed full of baseball trading card, comics, toys, and other collectible things.

. . . .

Hillbilly's BBQ & Steaks

720 McAdenville Road, Lowell, NC 28098 · (704) 824-8838
Monday–Saturday 11:00 A.M. –9:30 P.M.;
Sunday 11:00 P.M.–3:00 P.M.
www.hillbillysbbqsteaks.com

My friend Al Brand from Charlotte worked for many years at Pharr Yarns in nearby McAdenville. The textile plant is still thriving, a proud North Carolina tradition, and he told me that Hillbilly's was one of the favorite lunch spots for folks who worked at the mill.

You'll see what he means when you walk in and see the cheerful checkerboard country tablecloths and the tables filled with locals. The Boston butts are cooking over hickory wood coals inside, and the aroma is worth the price of the meal.

Owner Gerald Duncan explained to me that their barbecue is a combination of Lexington and Eastern North Carolina styles— with a tomato-based sauce that has a touch of vinegar. Maybe a "purist" would object, but not me. I found their combination mighty tasty. Duncan says, "Our menu and comfortable atmosphere create a truly enjoyable dining experience. We treat everyone like family."

FROM I-85 Take Exit 23 (Lowell/McAdenville). Hillbilly's is at the intersection. If you are coming from the north, you will almost drive into the parking lot as you drive up the exit ramp. If you come from the south, you will turn left at the end of the exit ramp onto McAdenville Rd. Then cross the overpass, and you will see Hillbilly's on the left.

AFTER EATING In December, downtown McAdenville is transformed, with hundreds of thousands of twinkling lights turning the town into a spectacular holiday display, drawing thousands of visitors every evening. Even at other times during the year, a visit to the restored McAdenville Historic District is worth a trip to see more than 100 contributing buildings and structures, including an upscale destination restaurant, a coffee and tea shop, an organic and natural foods grocer, an ice cream parlor, and a nostalgic hardware and mercantile store.

· ·

Catfish Cove

1401 Armstrong Ford Road, Belmont, NC 28012 · (704) 825-3332
Sunday (buffet) 11:00 A.M.–3:00 P.M.;
Tuesday–Thursday 4:00 P.M.–9:00 P.M.; Friday 4:00 P.M.–10:00 P.M.;
Saturday 3:00 P.M.–10:00 P.M.; closed Monday
MAY NOT ACCEPT CREDIT CARDS

Fish camp restaurants used to be a staple in Piedmont North Carolina, and people in Gaston and Mecklenburg Counties still talk about the joys of family meals at Lineberger's Fish Fry. Lineberger's is long gone, but Raymond Stowe, who cooked at Lineberger's for 30 years, has picked up the mantle at Catfish Cove, which he owns. Stowe knows how to get the oil at exactly the right temperature to seal the outside of the fish and hold the flavor inside. On the Friday night I visited, Stowe, his son, Kent, and Kent's wife, Summer, were busy getting seafood platters from the kitchen to the customers who had filled up the restaurant. But Raymond took time to smile with pride when he told me about how he took his savings from working at Lineberger's to build his own family business.

Sitting at the next table were Bobby Benton, Gray Brookshire, Ray Oehler, and their spouses. They live in the Mallard Creek section of Charlotte, and they told me, "We live a half-mile from a chain seafood restaurant, but we drive 30 miles every week to eat at Catfish Cove."

They were enjoying the catfish platter, which is what I am going for next time. I had the senior platter with scallops, fried onions, hushpuppies, and unlimited trips to the salad bar, all for much less than $10. But my new friends from Mallard Creek told me it was the catfish that they loved the most.

On Sunday, things change at Catfish Cove. At lunchtime, the fish camp stops serving seafood and becomes an all-you-can-eat country buffet.

FROM I-85 Take Exit 26 and follow Belmont-Mt. Holly Rd. toward Belmont. Go 0.5 mile and bear right onto Central Ave. After 0.8 mile turn right onto South Main St. and continue onto Armstrong Ford Rd. for 2 miles. Catfish Cove is on the left after you cross the river.

AFTER EATING Sit on the porch and enjoy the waters of the South Fork Catawba River. Less than 5 miles away is the much-admired Daniel Stowe Botanical Garden at 6500 South New Hope Rd. On your way back to I-85 (Exit 26) stop at the lovely campus of Belmont Abbey College, founded in 1876 by Benedictine monks and home to more than 1,700 students.

United House of Prayer for All People

2321 Beatties Ford Road, Charlotte, NC 28216 · (704) 394-3884
Monday–Friday 11:00 A.M.–7:00 P.M.;
Saturday 9:00 A.M.–3:00 P.M.; Sunday 10:00 A.M.–4:30 P.M.

The late Bishop C. M. "Daddy" Grace, founder of the national United House of Prayer for All People, would be proud of this mission service of his church. The modestly priced southern food is served cafeteria-style in friendly surroundings and happily satisfies most visitors. Some soul food fans say it delivers the very best fried chicken, meat loaf, cornbread, sweet potatoes, and cabbage around.

Sunday worship at the House of Prayer is enthusiastic, with a brass band accompanying singing and dancing. That enthusiasm carries over to mealtime.

FROM I-85 Take Exit 37 to Beatties Ford Rd. and turn right and go 0.5 mile. House of Prayer will be on the right.

AFTER EATING Ask for more information about the church and for a look at the main meeting hall. Also, Johnson C. Smith University Campus is 1.8 miles south at 100 Beatties Ford Rd.

Other nearby eateries described in the I-77 chapter include John's Family Restaurant, Lupie's Cafe, The Open Kitchen, Acropolis Cafe & Grille, and The Soda Shop.

Townhouse II

1870 South Main Street, Kannapolis, NC 28081 · (704) 938-8220
Monday–Friday 5:00 A.M.–6:00 P.M.; Saturday 5:00 A.M.–2:00 P.M.

You will have to turn a few corners to get there. But if you're looking for a place where the Concord and Kannapolis crowd gathers
for breakfast and lunch, or if you're looking for a place to get a good
country meal for a reasonable price, it's worth winding your way to
what the locals call "Janie's Townhouse II."

Be ready to eat. As one customer, Beth Snead, told me long ago,
"You had better be careful when you make your order. If you ask for
the 'large' plate and eat it all, you will be so full that you are just
going to want to crawl under your desk when you get back to work."

It is still true today.

UNC–Chapel Hill School of Medicine's Dr. Pete Chikes practiced in Concord for many years. When he goes back to visit, one of
his first stops is Townhouse II. "You can go in and see everybody
and interact with them, folks from all walks of life," he says. "And
the food is unbeatable."

Many years ago, when I first stopped by, it was the middle of
the afternoon. People were coming in, filling the place up. I wondered why they were there at that hour. The late Janie Hall, the
owner, explained that they were eating an early supper. They have
to eat early because Townhouse closes at 6:00 P.M. Why so early?
Well, to open at 5:00 A.M., Janie said she had to get up at 1:00 A.M.
and needed to get to bed early.

Everybody misses Janie, but her husband, Gene, her daughter,
Carmen Steen, and Carmen's daughter, Casey, all help keep the
restaurant going. In 2015, Casey had a baby, Kaylee Rebecca Price,
who is already visiting regularly and could become the family's
fourth-generation connection to Townhouse II.

FROM I-85 Take Exit 58 (Concord/Kannapolis). Take the Concord/
US 29 South ramp. Continue for 0.5 mile to US 29A (South Main St.).
Turn right and go 2 miles.

AFTER EATING When you pull up to Townhouse II, you will notice a sign beside the restaurant featuring a scantily clad woman. Don't look for any such entertainment inside. The sign simply advertises a lingerie shop in the adjoining shopping area. Why not make a quick visit and look for a present for a loved one?

· ·

Troutman's Bar-B-Q

362 Church Street, North Concord, NC 28025 · (704) 786-5213
Monday–Thursday 6:30 A.M.–8:30 P.M.; Friday 6:30 A.M.–9:00 P.M.;
Saturday 6:00 A.M.–9:00 P.M.; Sunday 7:00 A.M.–9:00 P.M.
www.letseat.at/troutmansbarbecue

Concord auto dealer and entrepreneur Raiford Troutman founded this institution more than 50 years ago. Now into his 90s, he still stops by daily to check things out and touch base with his daughter, Karen Barbie, who runs Troutman's the way her dad did. Both take pride in cooking barbecue the old-fashioned way. "We only use hickory wood to smoke our pork shoulders," she told me. "Our Pit Master slow cooks each shoulder for twelve hours. The smoke produced by the coals slowly seeps into the meat for a true, pit-cooked taste in every bite."

Their regulars like their red slaw, a mix of red and white cabbage with pimentos, tomatoes, and a sweetened vinegar-based dressing.

Troutman's at breakfast time is a popular place for regulars to gather and talk. What explains the crowds at breakfast? Maybe it is just a tradition. Maybe it is the full breakfast plates that some people promise are just as good as Troutman's wonderful barbecue.

Troutman's historic location is on Church St. in downtown Concord. There is a larger facility at 1388 Warren C. Coleman Blvd., near the intersection of US 601 and NC 49. But when Hillary Clinton came to Concord to campaign in 2008, she, like many candidates before and since, made a stop at the Church St. location.

Troutman's Bar-B-Q on Church Street in Concord

FROM I-85 Take Exit 58 toward Concord. Follow US 29/US 601 South (Cannon Blvd.) toward Concord. Go 1.3 miles. Bear right onto NC 73, which turns into Church St. Follow Church St. for 1.3 miles. Troutman's is on the left.

AFTER EATING Drive by the First Presbyterian Church, a few blocks away, at 70 Union St. Built in 1927, it was designed by Hobart Upjohn, who, according to Catherine Bishir, combined "red brick walls, simple forms and handsome classical detailing" in his work. It was an appropriate place for Charles A. Cannon to worship. During the 1920s, Mr. Cannon merged nine separate companies to form Cannon Mills Company. He built the world's largest household textile manufacturer, each day producing hundreds of thousands of Cannon towels.

Gary's Bar-B-Cue

620 North US 29, China Grove, NC 28023 · (704) 857-8314
Monday–Saturday 10:00 A.M.–9:30 P.M.; closed Sunday
MAY NOT ACCEPT CREDIT CARDS

Gary's Bar-B-Cue must be good, says Debbie Mullis of Concord, "because every time I'm there you'll usually find county patrolmen, National Guard personnel, and plenty of blue-collar workers alongside the coats and ties of businessmen."

She's right, and Gary's has been a stopping point on the road between Charlotte and Greensboro for a long time, even though finding it from the "new" I-85 can be a little bit confusing.

Gary's is really a museum of times gone by. He has a collection of old advertising signs that he displays on the walls. Incredibly, he always has an old-time, fully restored Chevrolet Corvette, Ford Thunderbird, Volkswagen bus, or other classic vehicle displayed on the floor of the restaurant.

Don't be misled by the sign on the side of Gary's building that says "Cokes 5¢." It is just a reminder of days gone by. But you do get free refills.

Gary specializes in barbecue, more or less Lexington style, and the crowds of people who visit there every day, both locals and travelers who somehow find their way from the interstate, show that Gary's barbecue is worth the trip.

Gary's does a big take-out business. It advertises a "Funeral Meal" with one-third pound of barbecue for each person, together with slaw, baked beans, and chips, for $6.50 a person. Twenty-five cents extra to add potato salad.

Once, when I paid my bill to my waitress at Gary's cash register, I asked if there were a senior citizens' discount. "Oh," she said, looking horrified, "there is, but once I've rung it up, it's too late."

Then she looked me sweetly in the eye and said, "You know, we're not allowed to ask folks if they are seniors even when they look old enough. Some people take offense. And, you, oh no! I never would have guessed."

She knew that she had made my day. I went back to the counter, left an extra tip, and walked out the door, holding my gray head high, a little bit giddy, thinking about Corvettes and drive-ins and days long gone by.

When I was back at Gary's recently on a Monday evening, the house was packed with cheerful eaters. Of course, I remembered to ask for my discount, and I got it.

FROM I-85 *If headed north:* Take Exit 68 (China Grove/Rockland/ NC 152). From the intersection, turn left onto NC 152 and head west for about 0.5 mile, following signs to US 29 Bypass/US 601 South and turning right on Madison Rd. as it loops around to US 29 Bypass/US 601 South. Follow US 29 Bypass/US 601 South for about a half-mile. Gary's is on the left.

If headed south: Take Exit 68 (China Grove/Rockland/US 29 Bypass South). From the intersection, follow US 29 Bypass South for about 1.5 miles. Gary's is on the left.

AFTER EATING Tiger World, a "fun and educational place to experience endangered species up close and personal," is about 10 minutes away at 4400 Cook Rd., Rockwell. Call (704) 279-6363 to schedule a visit or get information.

· ·

Porky's Bar-B-Q

1309 North Main Street, China Grove, NC 28023 · (704) 857-0400
Tuesday–Saturday 5:30 A.M.–9:00 P.M.;
Sunday 7:00 A.M.–9:00 P.M.; closed Monday

Porky's is only a minute or two from Gary's. Its current owner, Rick Register, is continuing the tradition of former owner Mike Reid, who insisted on cooking with wood, appealing to those barbecue fans who claim that it is not real barbecue if it is not "pit cooked."

Porky's takes its day off on Monday rather than Sunday, giving it a big edge on Sundays, when most of the barbecue places along I-85 are closed up tight. It also serves a variety of food other than barbecue, appealing to people who like home cooking but don't want to eat barbecue at every stop.

Finally, there is a matter of the slaw. As Elizabeth Cook, editor of the *Salisbury Post*, once told me, "It's the only barbecue place I know of around here that offers Carolina-style slaw—red, vinegary—and what I call Virginia slaw—sweet and mayonnaise-based—like I used to get back home in Fredericksburg."

You won't be able to find "Virginia slaw" at many other places around here. Though a few nearby Porky's have closed, the original is still going strong.

FROM I-85 *If headed north:* Take Exit 68 (China Grove/Rockland/ NC 152). From the intersection, turn left onto NC 152, head west for about 1 mile to the first stoplight (keep straight, being careful not to take any exits). At the stoplight, take a hard left turn onto Main St. Just after that turn you will see Porky's on the right.

If headed south: Take Exit 68 (China Grove/Rockland/US 29 Bypass South). From the intersection, follow US 29 Bypass South for about 1 mile, then take the exit marked NC 152/US 29 North. The exit ramp merges with Madison Rd. and then immediately intersects with NC 152/US 29 North. Turn right and follow this road for about 0.5 mile to a stoplight. At the stoplight, take a hard left turn onto Main Street. Just after that turn you will see Porky's on the right.

AFTER EATING For a nontraditional tourist stop, visit Copart Salvage Auto Auctions at nearby 1081 Recovery Rd. You will find a virtual museum of the history of American automobiles in all kinds of conditions. It is about a mile away via Main St.; turn right onto US 29 and then left on Madison.

Wink's King of Barbecue

509 Faith Road, Salisbury, NC 28146 · (704) 637-2410
Monday–Saturday 5:30 A.M.–9:00 P.M.; closed Sunday

Wink's is convenient to I-85, only about one-half mile from the exit. Located on Faith Rd., it greets you with a "You are blessed" sign and a motto of "Where good people meet for good food." Wink's gives you more of a regular local home cooking experience than the barbecue name on its sign would indicate. The barbecue is good, but some customers are more likely to praise the biscuit and gravy breakfast offerings with fresh local sausage. Breakfast is always available, and the homemade pimento cheese is also a specialty.

The same family has operated Wink's since Dwight and Iris Martin opened it in 1955. It moved to its current location in 2001 and is managed by the Martins' daughter, Dinah Cordell. You can trust Wink's to bless you with a square meal all day long.

FROM I-85 Take Exit 76 to merge onto US 52 South/E. Innes St. toward Albemarle. Go 0.2 mile. Turn right onto Faith Rd. Go 0.4 mile. Wink's will be on the right.

AFTER EATING Nearby is Old Stone House, constructed in 1766, when the site was wilderness, by German immigrant Michael Braun. Catherine Bishir writes that the massive, two-story house is "the principal surviving example of early Germanic architecture outside of Salem." My close friend and Salisbury native Wyndham Robertson remembers the many school field trips she took to the site, maybe enough, she says, "for a lifetime." The house is only 2.5 miles from Wink's by way of US 52 South (East Innes St.). Turn left on Dunn's Mountain Church Rd. and then right on Old Stone House Rd.

Richard's Bar B-Q

522 North Main Street, Salisbury, NC 28144 · (704) 636-9561
Monday–Saturday 6:00 A.M.–8:00 P.M.; closed Sunday
MAY NOT ACCEPT CREDIT CARDS

Owner Richard Monroe has been hand-chopping barbecue here since 1979, when he became the manager for the former owners. He changed the name when he took over ownership. Barbecue expert Jim Early writes that Richard's barbecue has "a good smoky pork flavor and deep smoke penetration from the slow roasting."

The flavor comes from Richard's real pit, real wood, and real smoke.

Richard's is a local gathering place, and I like it for the same reason as Walter Turner, former historian at the nearby transportation museum in Spencer. He told me he enjoys Richard's "comfortable, cozy atmosphere with nice booths and waitresses that keep my iced tea glass full."

Breakfast at Richard's is popular in Salisbury, in part because it is one place where local livermush lovers can get their fix.

FROM I-85 Take Exit 76 and head west into Salisbury. Follow East Innes St. (US 52) into Salisbury for 1 mile. Turn right onto North Main St. and go 0.5 mile. Richard's is on the left.

AFTER EATING Visit the Rowan Museum in the impressive Old County Courthouse a few blocks away at 202 North Main St. From the Old Courthouse visit the Salisbury National Cemetery, originally established by Confederate authorities to serve as the burial ground for thousands of captured Union soldiers who died while incarcerated at the prison in Salisbury. The Federal Monument to the Unknown Dead, a 50-foot-high granite obelisk, honors the unknown Union soldiers who died in the prison. To get there, follow North Main St. for 0.4 mile and turn left on East Monroe St. Go for 0.2 mile and turn on South Railroad St. and then left on Government Rd. and follow it to the cemetery.

College Barbecue

117 Statesville Boulevard, Salisbury, NC 28144 · (704) 633-9953
Monday 7:00 A.M.–2:00 P.M.; Tuesday–Friday 7:00 A.M.–8:00 P.M.;
Saturday 7:00 A.M.–3:00 P.M.; Sunday 7:00 A.M.–8:00 P.M.

College Barbecue is a popular gathering place, especially at break-fast and lunch. Lots of faithful fans in Salisbury appreciate the chopped pork shoulders that have been cooked over hickory coals for hours and hours. The day I stopped by, owner Jay Owen and son Jason were building a shed for their hickory wood. Jay explained that the wood storage room in the restaurant was being converted into a second barbecue cooker needed due to increased demand on special occasions. Then he took me inside to show me the shoulders slowly cooking to be ready the next day.

Jay's uncle, David Koontz, opened College Barbecue in the 1960s and sold it to Jay in 1998. Jay and Jason and the other folks at College work to make you feel like you're back in a small-town eatery of 50 years ago. Their hushpuppies, sweet tea, soups, and French fries complement the wood-smoked barbecue.

FROM I-85 Take Exit 76 and head west into Salisbury. Follow East Innes St. (US 52) into Salisbury and as it turns into West Innes St. for 2.5 miles to an intersection with Statesville Blvd. on the right and Mahaley Ave. on the left. Turn right onto Statesville Blvd. College Bar-B-Que will be on the left.

AFTER EATING Drive by the nearby W. G. (Bill) Hefner VA Medical Center, a 484-bed facility at 1601 Brenner Ave., where countless veterans, including my father who died there in 1974, have been well treated and cared for. Catawba College, alma mater of Governor Pat McCrory, is just a few blocks away on Innes St.

College Barbecue in Salisbury

....

Backcountry Barbeque

4014 Linwood-Southmont Road, Linwood, NC 27299
(336) 956-1696
Monday–Saturday 6:00 A.M.–9:00 P.M.; Sunday 11:00 A.M.–9:00 P.M.

Backcountry is our last Lexington-area barbecue stop if you are
going south on I-85—and the first if you are headed north. First or
last, it is a good stop to make. There is a big woodpile in the back,
and pork shoulders are cooking all the time.

My friend Grant McRorie told me that Backcountry might look
bad on the outside, but the barbecue on the inside was mighty good.
He was right on both counts.

Doug Cook, the owner, has done so well that he is able to spend
most of his time in Colorado these days writing and performing
music. But he has assembled a capable crew led by his stepdaughter,

Christy Hunt, to cook and prepare the barbecue every day. One of the crew showed me how the pork is cooked all day over coals, then kept warm with the help of electric cookers overnight to keep the barbecue from being too moist. Then I saw how they pull the fresh cooked meat from the bone and rough chop it just after the customer places an order.

All in all, a visit here is worth the little extra effort it takes to find it.

FROM I-85 Take Exit 88 (Linwood). (Be careful, and don't get confused. The road names and addresses are a jumble. But it is close to the intersection and you can find it.) From the intersection, head east on NC 47 toward Linwood. Go about 0.8 mile. Backcountry Barbeque is on the right across the road from a former furniture manufacturing plant.

. . . .

Lexington Barbecue, Lexington

100 Smokehouse Lane, Lexington, NC 27295 · (336) 249-9814
Monday–Saturday 10:00 A.M.–9:30 P.M.; closed Sunday
(and most "Monday holidays" and for a week around July 4)

Lexington Barbecue is always busy and crowded. You will find locals and people from all over the state and beyond in line at mealtimes. But they never have to wait long—and they never feel rushed to finish. Owner Wayne Monk has a formula that gets food to the table quickly and keeps his customers happy.

I usually get a chopped tray with slaw, hushpuppies, and sweet iced tea. The food is very good, but what keeps me coming back is the way the waitresses take such good care of me—filling up my tea, getting more hushpuppies, smiling, and sometimes slipping and calling me "hon." "Need anything else, hon?" they ask.

I have been there so many times that I think Wayne Monk recognizes me when I come in. But even when I first started eating there and nobody knew me, they still treated me like I was part of the family.

When I leave, I am a few dollars poorer and feel a million dollars better. I think I would feel that way even if the food were not so good. But the barbecue, slaw, and hushpuppies are judged by the experts to be outstanding.

According to Jack Betts, former *Charlotte Observer* associate editor, Lexington Barbecue is "regarded by many travelers as the Mother Church of N.C. barbecue."

Bob Garner, author of *North Carolina Barbecue: Flavored by Time*, also uses religious terms to describe this place: "To the faithful, all roads still lead to Lexington Barbecue."

Barbecue insiders often refer to the restaurant and to Wayne Monk as "Honeymonk." I always wondered where such a name came from. Wayne explained that when he decided to open his own place, he borrowed $500 and got his brother-in-law, Sonny Honeycutt, to invest more and become an equal partner. Sonny had a sign made combining the two names, "Honeymonk's."

Wayne says he never approved, and the sign is now long gone, because Sonny quickly had enough of the barbecue business and left after three months.

In 2015, *USA Today* included Skylight Inn and Lexington Barbecue in their list of "10 Best Southern Barbecue Spots." So even if you have never eaten here, it should be your first stop, even though it is several miles from I-85.

FROM I-85 *If headed north:* Take Exit 87 onto I-85 Business. Go 1.2 miles and take the second exit from the right lane onto US 64 West toward Mocksville. Go 0.1 mile and turn left onto West Center St. Go 0.1 mile and turn left onto West Center St. Ext. Go 0.2 mile and turn left onto Smokehouse Ln. Lexington Barbecue will be on the right.

If headed south: Take Exit 96 for US 64 toward Lexington/Asheboro. Turn right onto US 64. Go 5.2 miles and make a very sharp right onto Smokehouse Ln. Lexington Barbecue will be on the left. (Watch out! The turn onto Smokehouse Ln. is tricky and not even noted by some map services. Keep a lookout on the right. Just before the turn you will pass a park and then cross an overpass, which is just before the right turn onto Smokehouse Ln.)

AFTER EATING Walk around the side of the restaurant to get a look at the chimneys rising above the pit and, if you are lucky, get a whiff of the flavored smoke that comes out when the pork shoulders are cooking. If you have the courage, ask Rick Monk or another family member to show you the inside of the pit.

. . . .

Bar-B-Q Center

900 North Main Street, Lexington, NC 27292 · (336) 248-4633
Monday–Saturday 6:00 A.M.–9:00 P.M.; closed Sunday
www.facebook.com/barbecuecenter

Lots of people thought Sonny Conrad's wood-cooked pork was the best they have ever had. When he died in July 2013, Sharon Myers wrote in the *Lexington Dispatch* that his "influence has effortlessly spread throughout the community from the tireless work ethic he showed through example to the one-on-one relationships he built with his customers and his role as a pioneer of the largest one-day festival in North Carolina, the Barbecue Festival."

With the founder of the restaurant gone, some people worried about its future. But the family and especially his wife, Nancy, and their two sons, Cecil and Michael, had been working in the business most of their lives. The family is continuing Sonny's traditions.

If you are willing to get a little farther off the main roads and make your way to downtown Lexington, you ought to try the food at Bar-B-Q Center. Some people rate the Conrads' wood-cooked pork as the best around.

You don't think about barbecue and ice cream making a good mix. But here they do. The restaurant started as a dairy bar, and you can still get a banana split or other ice cream treats to go with your barbecue.

FROM I-85 Take Exit 96 toward US 64/Lexington/Asheboro and go 4 miles. Then keep left onto North Main St. (US 29-BR/US 70-BR) toward Lexington/Downtown. Go 0.4 mile. Bar-B-Q Center is on the right.

AFTER EATING Follow Main St. to downtown and visit some of the stores, like the Army-Navy Store at 14 North Main St. Note that it features new specialty clothing and does not sell military surplus.

. . . .

Southern Lunch

26 South Railroad Street, Lexington, NC 27292 · (336) 248-5276
Tuesday–Friday 7:00 A.M.–8:00 P.M.;
Saturday 7:00 A.M.–12:00 P.M. (breakfast only);
Sunday 7:00 A.M.–3:00 P.M.; closed Monday

I was looking for a regular home-style restaurant in this barbecue town, and former Davidson County Board of Commissioners chairman Tommy Hedrick told me about Southern Lunch being a favorite of his because "Everybody goes." Tommy loves the stew beef and scalloped tomatoes. Jack Briggs, owner of several funeral homes in the region, is a regular at lunch to get his favorites, which he says are "lima beans, scalloped tomatoes, and sweet potatoes."

Others praise the breakfast offerings and the chicken and dumplings, country fried steak, sweet potatoes, meat loaf, and chicken pot pie.

Tommy Hedrick likes the friendly waitresses, the downtown location, and its owner, Herb Lohr. Herb is the third-generation owner of the business, started in 1925 near the old railroad depot. When I asked Lohr who would take over when he retired, he said, "I'm not thinking about that. I am going to be here until I die, just like my dad and my granddad. Most people don't have the opportunity to do what they were meant to do. My life has been great." Lohr gives his wife, Windy, and his love of sports credit for his happiness.

I asked Lohr why, in Lexington, the home of barbecue, there was no mention of it on his menu. His answer came quickly: "My granddad said, 'Everybody else has barbecue. I am not going to have it.'"

FROM I-85 Take Exit 94 and follow Old US 64 (Old Raleigh Rd.) toward Lexington. In about 0.5 mile bear left onto East Center St. Ext. Follow East Center St. Ext. and East Center St. for about 3.5 miles to South Railroad St. Turn left on South Railroad St. and Southern Lunch will be on the right.

AFTER EATING Be sure to see the giant mural in the restaurant. It depicts life in downtown Lexington as it was in 1925 when the railroad was king. Then check out some of the special downtown retailers, like Conrad & Hinkle Food Market a few blocks away at 6 North Main St. Established in 1919 by W. E. Conrad and E. Odell Hinkle, it has grown into one of the state's most respected specialty food stores. People come from miles away to buy the special pimento cheese, made with American cheese rather than cheddar. At 2 South Main St. is the Davidson County Historical Museum in the old 1856 courthouse, which was modeled on the Virginia state capitol.

On your way back to I-85, visit the Bob Timberlake Gallery at 1714 East Center St. Ext.

. . . .

Tommy's Bar-B-Que

206 National Highway, Thomasville, NC 28360 · (336) 476-4322
Monday–Saturday 6:00 A.M.–9:00 P.M.; closed Sunday

The barbecue in nearby Lexington gets most of the attention, and barbecue experts often overlook what is going on in nearby Thomasville. The locals, however, swear by the barbecue and other good food that Tommy Everhart has been cooking since the 1970s. In 1970, he started out as a "curb boy" at the restaurant, which was then called Blackwelder's. He later bought Blackwelder's and changed the name to Tommy's.

I loved the friendly service and the reminder that I was eligible for the 10 percent senior's discount. Tommy Everhart has retired, too. Sort of. He stops by to help his daughters Tammy Todd, the current manager, and Belinda Smith. As you wind your way around downtown to get to Tommy's, don't forget to take a look at the famous Thomasville giant chair as you cross the railroad tracks.

FROM I-85 Take Exit 103 (Thomasville/NC 109). Head north on NC 109 (Randolph St.). Go 1.8 miles on Randolph St., and, after crossing the railroad tracks, turn right onto East Main St. and go 0.6 mile. Turn left onto National Hwy. Go 0.2 mile. Tommy's is on the left.

AFTER EATING Make your way back to Main St. to get another look at the giant chair. Take a photo of your group. Visit the nearby 1870 train depot at 44 West Main St., now the home of the Thomasville Visitors' Center. Catherine Bishir notes the "fanciful sawnwork frieze beneath the eaves giving an unmistakably stylish note."

· ·

Captain Tom's Seafood Restaurant

1037 Randolph Street, Thomasville, NC 27360 · (336) 476-6563
Tuesday–Thursday 11:00 A.M.–8:30 P.M.; Friday 4:00 P.M.–9:30 P.M.;
Saturday 11:00 A.M.–9:30 P.M.; Sunday 12:00 P.M.–9:30 P.M.;
closed Monday

Need a break from barbecue and home-style cooking? Got a hankering to visit one of those old-time fish camps? If so, Captain Tom's might be the right place for you. It serves the traditional broiled and fried seafood platters at reasonable prices—even more reasonable at lunchtime.

Florence Matthews eats there two or three times a week. When I told her that I thought Captain Tom's was pretty good, she looked me in the eye and said severely that it was more than "pretty good. It's a lot better than what they've got at the beach."

From the crowd of people in Captain Tom's that day, I would guess that a lot of folks agree with Ms. Matthews.

FROM I-85 Take Exit 103 (Thomasville/NC 109). From the intersection, head north on NC 109 (Randolph St.) toward Thomasville. Go about 0.5 mile. Captain Tom's is on the right.

AFTER EATING On weekends visit the Eleven Acre Flea Market at 825 Julian Ave. about 0.5 mile away; follow Randolph St. and bear right onto Julian Ave.

....

Pioneer Family Restaurant and Steakhouse

10914 North Main Street, Archdale, NC 27263 · (336) 861-6247
Monday–Thursday 11:00 A.M.–9:00 P.M.;
Friday–Sunday 10:00 A.M.–9:30 P.M.

The Pioneer Family Restaurant and Steakhouse has built a long-standing tradition of providing a full plate of country cooking and a great community gathering place. It's almost always packed with locals. You can order from a menu of charbroiled steaks, seafood, and sandwiches, but almost everybody goes to the 80-item buffet bar for a near-unlimited selection. It is a bargain in the evenings and on Sunday, and an even better deal at lunch from 11:00 A.M. to 3:00 P.M. on weekdays and Saturday.

My old friend Johnny Bailey lives nearby. He and his wife go several times a week. "Why so often?" I asked him.

"Well, I guess it's because we're gluttons," he said before he could think. "No don't print that. My wife will kill me."

I hope she doesn't. But lots of people say that the buffet at the Pioneer is worth dying for. In 1987, Mike Liner and a partner opened Pioneer, eventually building the restaurant into a community institution. In 1993, then-congressman Howard Coble visited as part of a free luncheon for seniors. In the *Congressional Record* he reported that Mike gave "a place mat to each arriving senior citizen containing the seven rules which had to be followed in order to obtain a free meal. Those rules were: (1) No swinging from the chandeliers; (2) No dancing on tables; (3) No spitting tobacco juice on the floor; (4) No fist fights; (5) No food fights; (6) Police will be called for violators of the above rules; (7) Enjoy yourself. I can attest that all the rules, particularly No. 7, were observed with delight."

Mike sold the Pioneer in 1997 and ended up buying it back in 2009, after the owner decided to close up shop. Liner and his wife, Kathy, came back as owners, bringing their daughter, Misty Austin, to help them manage. Kathy passed away in 2013, and her portrait and a loving tribute are on display as a reminder of how she helped build, and then rebuild, the Pioneer tradition.

Mike's advice for others going into business: "Do something you love and don't do it for the money." Sounds right to me.

FROM I-85 Take Exit 111 (High Point/Archdale). From the intersection, head west on NC 311 (Main St.) toward High Point. Go about 1 mile. The Pioneer Family Restaurant and Steakhouse is on the right.

AFTER EATING Across the street at 10935 North Main St. is Mommy & Me Consignment, winner of an award for the best children's clothing store in town.

· ·

Mary B's Southern Kitchen

3529 Archdale Road, Archdale, NC 27263 · (336) 861-5964
Monday–Friday 11:00 A.M.–2:30 P.M.; closed Saturday–Sunday

Mary Bunn started the restaurant in 1987. She sold it to Janet Thomas, who, with her husband, Alvin, has been running Mary B's since 1992.

"Just for lunch," she says. "And only on weekdays."

She continues, "We serve traditional southern food the way you remember it. This is the comfort food you grew up with. We don't believe in cutting corners here. If we wouldn't serve it to our family, we figure it's not good enough to serve to you. Come in, grab a chair, and you'll be a regular before you know it!"

Alvin says Janet's chicken pot pie, cooked the Moravian way without vegetables, is his and the customers' favorite. But Laura Cromer told me she comes in at least once a week just for the meat loaf. Regular customer Mark Rumley, who owns Bush Hill Trading Post (beside the Days Inn at Exit 111), swears by the fried chicken.

The food is served cafeteria-style, which appeals to customers in a hurry. But most visitors prefer to linger and enjoy Janet's and Alvin's warm hospitality.

FROM I-85 Take Exit 111 (High Point/Archdale). From the intersection, head west on NC 311 (Main St.) toward High Point. Go about 1 mile. Turn left on NC 62. Go about 0.5 mile. Turn left onto Archdale Rd. Mary B's will be on the left in a small shopping center.

AFTER EATING One block away, on Trindale Rd., there are a couple of consignment shops that are worth a look, including PJ's Consignment at 311 Trindale Rd.

. . . .

Kepley's Bar-B-Q

1304 North Main Street, High Point, NC 27262 · (336) 884-1021
Monday–Saturday 10:00 A.M.–8:30 P.M.; closed Sunday
www.kepleysbarbecue.com

Is Kepley's worth a side trip from the interstate? You will get a definite "yes" from almost everybody who grew up in High Point, where Kepley's is a community institution that brings back many happy memories. Kepley's is plain and simple, just like it has been since 1948 when it opened. That might be the secret of its success. Or maybe it is their special vinegar-based and pepper-flavored barbecue that has kept people coming back for almost 70 years.

Chapel Hill lawyer Bob Epting grew up in High Point. He says Kepley's barbecue sandwich makes his mouth and his heart "fly back fifty years, to our '57 Chevys and Fords. Kepley's vinegar-based barbeque and slaw are just that unique. I guarantee you will never have had a better barbeque treat, certainly not one that works its magic in your memory, taking you home again to memories of hurried conversations with pals about which girl you wished you had the courage to call, and their long lost but still familiar faces."

After those lovely memories, how could anyone not stop by to experience Kepley's?

In 1948, Hayden Kepley started selling barbecue in an old army Quonset hut. In 1962, Kepley retired and sold Kepley's Bar-B-Q to his son-in-law, Charlie Johnson, and Bob Burleson, who had worked as a curb boy since he was age 16. They worked together for many years, and now Burleson is the sole owner.

FROM I-85 *If headed north:* Take Exit 111 onto Main St./US 311 South toward High Point and go 6 miles. Kepley's is just before Main intersects Lexington Ave.

If headed south: Take Exit 118 and follow I-85 Business toward High Point for 7 miles. Exit onto Main St. (US 311) and go toward High Point for 3 miles. Kepley's is just before Main intersects Lexington Ave.

AFTER EATING Next door at 1300 North Main St. is the 12,000-square-foot showroom of High Point Furniture Finds, which bills itself as "North Carolina's best discount furniture store." Bob Epting suggests a visit to High Point Central High School's building, just a shady 4-block walk. Completed in 1926 and designed by Greensboro architect Harry Barton in Collegiate Gothic style, it was considered the grandest educational building in the state.

Other nearby eateries, including Stamey's Old Fashioned Barbecue and Smith Street Diner, are described in the I-40 chapter.

Jack's Barbecue

213 West Main Street, Gibsonville, NC 27249 · (336) 449-6347
Monday–Saturday 11:00 A.M.–7:00 P.M.
(closing a little earlier on Wednesday and Saturday); closed Sunday

Jack's is small and a little bit out of the way. But the folks are so nice, and downtown Gibsonville is a wonderful slice of small-town North Carolina.

The food is good, too. They like to brag about their special, Jack's Big Boy, a giant burger with lettuce, tomatoes, onions, mayonnaise, mustard, and melted cheese. If it sounds like something you could get at the fast food place, believe me when I say that it really tastes quite different, quite wonderful—just like the hamburgers at your favorite place back home.

In 1967, Jack Rook bought Henry's Barbecue, where he had been working. He changed the name to Jack's, which moved to its current location in 1970. Jack's daughter Kathy Sykes is the owner. Another daughter, Jacki Allison, is manager.

If you're lucky, famous Gibsonville natives like former N.C. State and NFL football player Torry Holt could drop by. Another native, the late N.C. State women's basketball coach Kay Yow, was a regular when she came back home. Check out the displays about Holt, Yow, and other Gibsonville heroes.

FROM I-85 Take Exit 138. Head north on NC 61. Go about 3 miles to where this road intersects with West Main St. in downtown Gibsonville. Turn right on West Main, and Jack's is on the right.

AFTER EATING Spend some time on Main St., including a visit to Wade's Jewelers, located at 101 East Main St. in a palatial building, inside and out. Stop by Once upon a Chocolate at 139 Piedmont Ave. to see an unbelievable display of chocolates made on-site. At 137 Piedmont Ave. is Pete's Grill, another favorite local eatery. For a wonderful, lifelike model train display, stop by Bobby's World of Trains at 113 Lewis St.

Jack's Barbecue in Gibsonville

··

Hursey's Pig-Pickin' Bar-B-Q

1834 South Church Street, Burlington, NC 27215 · (336) 226-1694
Monday–Saturday 11:00 A.M.–9:00 P.M.; closed Sunday

I would stop at Hursey's just for the great smells of burning hickory wood coming out of its chimneys all day long. Inside, I like to look at the gallery of people who have told Charlie Hursey that his barbecue is among the "best": Presidents Reagan, Clinton, and the first Bush; Senator Helms and Governor Hunt. Hursey says he usually votes Republican in presidential races, but he is proud to serve presidents and politicians of all parties.

Hursey's can trace its beginnings to 1945 when Sylvester Hursey and his wife, Daisy, began combining a special sauce with his father's method of cooking pork.

Charlie got his start working for his parents as a carhop. He joined the business full time in 1960.

Hursey's is home to a big take-out business. There is also a small, comfortable seating area. The menu is limited to barbecue and fried seafood. Hursey's fans, like the *Charlotte Observer*'s Jack Betts, swear that Hursey's is one of the best barbecue stops in the state.

In my book, Hursey's wins the hushpuppy contest, with its fresh, golden, crispy cakes that are sweet enough to be dessert.

FROM I-85 Take Exit 143. Head north on NC 62 (Alamance Rd.). Go about 1 mile to where this road intersects with NC 70 (Church St.). Hursey's is on the left at this intersection.

AFTER EATING The Alamance County Historical Museum is located on part of a 1,693-acre grain plantation, known in the nineteenth century as Oak Grove. The plantation was owned by three generations of the Holt family, pioneers in the textile business as early as 1837. Follow NC 62 south for about 5 miles to 4777 NC 62. Call ahead at (336) 226-8254.

· ·

Angelo's Family Restaurant

202 South Main Street #H, Graham, NC 27253 · (336) 227-6344
Monday–Saturday 11:00 A.M.–9:00 P.M.;
Sunday 11:00 A.M.–8:00 P.M.

Chapel Hill lawyer and pilot Bob Epting calls Angelo's Family Restaurant "The Church of Joanne." Joanne Rich, along with her brother Robbie, owns and operates Angelo's. Bob describes the restaurant as a "wonderful Italian diner famous for great spaghetti and meatballs, calzones, pizza, and the freshest salads and homemade dressings anywhere."

Bob continues, "It is usually crowded with local tradesmen, practicing professionals, thirsty softballers, landed pilots and 'friends of Joanne' of all age groups and social affiliations. Her red sauce, prepared on-site according to a generations-old family recipe, is alone worth the price of whatever you order."

Sure enough, when I visited the modestly furnished restaurant, I got the biggest and best calzone I have ever tried to eat. Delicious, but much more than I could finish. I took it home and it fed me lunch for two days.

FROM I-85 Take Exit 147 and follow NC 87 north for about a mile. Angelo's is in a shopping center on the right.

AFTER EATING Inspect two historic houses across Main St.: first, the Williamson House, at 141 South Main St., built about 1878 and restored for use by Bank of America; second, the Captain James White home, 213 S. Main St., built about 1873 and currently occupied by Alamance Arts, the local arts council, which provides a venue for the changing exhibitions and a location for Picasso's Gift Shop.

Other nearby eateries Allen & Son and
Margaret's Cantina are described in the I-40 chapter.

··

Hillsborough BBQ Company

236 South Nash Street, Hillsborough, NC 27278 · (919) 732-4647
Tuesday–Thursday 11:30 A.M.–9:00 P.M.;
Friday–Saturday 11:30 A.M.–10:00 P.M.;
Sunday 11:30 A.M.–9:00 P.M. closed Monday
hillsboroughbbq.com

Hillsborough BBQ Company is not a longtime, family-owned operation like almost every other restaurant in this collection. But it has something that only a few barbecue restaurants have: a real old-time pit where they cook pork butts over wood coals made from handpicked hickory and oak. The management-ownership team of Tommy Stann and Joel Bohlin has local folks singing praises. For instance, my dentist Sam Nesbit, who lives in Hillsborough, is a big fan and says he's never been disappointed. In addition to enjoying the good food, he says, "if tables are full, or if you happen to be by yourself, there is always a TV in the corner and a congenial crowd at the bar."

UNC-Chapel Hill provost Jim Dean and his wife, Jan, are big fans of local home cooking, and they put Hillsborough BBQ at the top of their list of favorites. Lee Smith, North Carolina's beloved

Joel Bohlin and Tommy Stan of Hillsborough BBQ Company in Hillsborough

author and a former owner of Akai Hana, a wonderful Japanese restaurant in Carrboro, tells me she eats at Hillsborough BBQ at least three times a week.

FROM I-85 Take Exit 164 and follow South Churton St. for 1.5 miles. Turn left onto West Margaret St. Go 1 mile. Turn left on South Nash. Go 1 block.

AFTER EATING Walk 2 blocks on Calvin St. to the entrance to Hillsborough's River Walk, which runs through the town and connects to the Mountains-to-Sea Trail. Use it to go for a short walk or bike ride along the Eno River.

Bennett Pointe Grill & Bar

4625 Hillsborough Road, Durham, NC 27705 · (919) 382-9431
Monday–Friday 11:30 A.M.–9:30 P.M.;
Saturday 5:00 P.M.–9:30 P.M.; Sunday 12:00 P.M.–8:00 P.M.
www.bpgrill.com

"We are so lucky. We just pray that it will never close," Janet Wells told me when I interrupted her quiet lunch with her sister at the Bennett Pointe Grill & Bar. "We live nearby, so we come here often. It is like home." Her 90-plus-year-old mother comes often, too, and always orders her favorite, chicken salad.

Friendly, longtime employees like Roslyn Evans (13 years) and Ashley Sealy (16 years) told me they enjoy getting to know their customers.

Bennett Pointe might be a little bit more upscale in décor and price than the usual neighborhood eatery, but it has found a formula that virtually guarantees a good experience for regulars like Janet Wells and visitors like me.

In 1997, when Lisa and Jonathan Lark first opened their restaurant, it had only 60 seats. Since then it has expanded and seats 160, including a full-service bar. The menu, at both lunch and supper, is varied with soups, salads, and sandwiches, and entrées of meats and seafood are available along with daily specials.

FROM I-85 *If headed north:* Take Exit 170 and follow US 70 Business for about 2 miles. Bennett Pointe will be on the right, next door to Food Lion in a shopping center.

If headed south: Take Exit 173 (Cole Mill Rd.) and follow Cole Mill Rd. for 0.3 miles. Then turn right onto Hillsborough Rd. (US 15-501) and go about 2 miles. Bennett Pointe will be on the left, next door to Food Lion in a shopping center.

AFTER EATING Visit Bennett Place Historic Site, where the largest troop surrender of the American Civil War took place. It is just a short walk or drive from the restaurant along Bennett Place Memorial Dr., which runs behind the shopping center. In the simple farmhouse, Confederate General Joseph E. Johnston and Union General William T. Sherman negotiated for several days and, on April 26, 1865, signed a surrender agreement like the one signed more than two weeks earlier at Appomattox.

Another restaurant, Backyard BBQ Pit, is close
by and described in the I-40 chapter.

. . . .

Bullock's Bar-B-Cue

3330 Quebec Drive, Durham, NC 27705 · (919) 383-3211
Tuesday–Saturday 11:30 A.M.–8:00 P.M.; closed Sunday–Monday
www.bullocksbbq.com

Bullock's may be the oldest continuously operating restaurant in Durham. It's where I got the idea to write this very book.

I was hungry, not just hungry for anything, but hungry for home cooking. In that city, I knew what to do. I headed for Bullock's. The lunchtime rush was long over, but it was still full. After I got settled in a booth, the waitress came up from behind me. I could hear her smiling as she said, "How you doing, hon?"

I had never seen the woman before, but she called me "hon."

For just a second I was the happiest man in the world. I knew that this woman, Sue Clements, was going to bring me a glass of sweet tea and keep it full the whole time I was there. She was going to treat me like we had been good friends forever.

Happy as I was, I started worrying about all those other people driving up and down I-40 and I-85, just a few miles away. Some of them, I thought, are just as hungry for a home-style meal as I am. They would love to be called "hon" and have their tea glasses kept full by Sue Clements. I knew I should seek out and share Bullock's and other home cooking places with you and others.

If somebody like Sue Clements keeps your glass filled with

sweet tea, what more do you need to say about Bullock's? But some of Bullock's fans will insist on telling you, "Everybody in Durham goes there."

It's true. A few minutes after Sue Clements filled my glass a second time, Susan Hester and Tonia Butler came in for a late lunch. We had worked together while I was on an interim assignment at North Carolina Central University.

They sensed that I was surprised to see them. "But D. G., didn't you know we always come to Bullock's?" Susan asked. "We come here all the time."

"I came to get me some fresh vegetables because I need something healthy," said Tonia Butler. But when she saw my barbecue, fried chicken, Brunswick stew, slaw, hushpuppies, and sweet tea, she laughed and told Sue Clements, "Same as he got."

She told me, "The healthy stuff will just have to wait."

Celebrities come here, too. Susan told me, "Shirley Caesar," the gospel singer and minister, "eats here all the time." On the way out, I saw a whole wall full of photos of famous people who ate at Bullock's.

But none could have eaten much happier than I did.

Owner Tommy Bullock's dad, Glen, started cooking barbecue for friends in the 1940s and opened Bullock's in 1952. Tommy and his family have owned and operated the business since 1965, at its current location since 1970.

FROM I-85 *If headed north:* Take Exit 173. Turn right onto Cole Mill Rd. Go 0.2 mile. Turn left on Hillsborough Rd. Go 0.6 mile to LaSalle St. Turn left. (You will see a big Rite-Aid on the corner.) Go one block to Quebec St. Bullock's is on the right.

If headed south: Take Exit 174B (you will exit to the left) and then be prepared for the Hillsborough Rd. exit, which comes up immediately on the right. Turn left on Hillsborough Rd. Go 0.6 mile to LaSalle St. on the left. Turn left here. (You will see a big Rite-Aid on the corner.) Go 1 block to Quebec St. Bullock's is on the right.

AFTER EATING Duke University's campus, which includes the chapel, the Nasher Art Museum, and the Sarah Duke gardens, is so close. But if you have just a few minutes, drive through the East

Campus site of Trinity College. It is only 2 miles from Bullock's along Hillsborough Rd. and Main St.

. . . .

Saltbox Seafood Joint

608 North Mangum Street, Durham, NC 27701 · (919) 908-8970
Tuesday–Saturday 11:00 A.M.–7:00 P.M. (or until the fish runs out);
closed Sunday–Monday

Saltbox Seafood Joint breaks all the guidelines for this book. It has not been around for long time. There is no dining room. It is mostly a stand-up place. But the modest surroundings do not deter loyal customers, folks from all over, from lining up beside this modest food stand with outdoor seating near Durham's Little Five Points.

The reason is owner Ricky Moore, who has been training for success in his own food business all his life. He grew up catching and cooking fish in eastern North Carolina. He cooked during his seven years in the army, studied at the Culinary Institute of America, and worked at the fine Glasshalfull restaurant in Carrboro and as the opening executive chef at Georgio's in Cary.

Moore features seafood including shrimp, salmon, trout, monkfish, catfish, soft-shell crab, tuna, and more, but only if it is freshly caught. It's good, but it is not as inexpensive as the surroundings might indicate. As Moore explained to me, he has to take into account that "the value is in the quality of fresh product we provide. Good, fresh seafood is not cheap, and the North Carolina fishermen deserve to get top dollar for their catch."

Even more value, however, is in the flavors that come from Moore's iron skillet, which caught the attention of *Saveur*: "The preparations reveal chef Ricky Moore's creativity and skill: toothsome grilled bluefish in a smoky-spicy rub of paprika and Aleppo pepper; an oyster roll, the plump, sweet mollusks dusted in fine cornmeal before frying, then topped with a fresh herb-laced slaw. Moore's tiny but mighty Saltbox . . . fulfills our wildest fantasies of what a takeout fish shack can be."

Ricky Moore of Saltbox Seafood Joint in Durham (photo by Baxter Miller)

FROM I-85 Take Exit 177 and follow US 501 Business South onto Roxboro St. headed into Durham. Then follow US 501 Business along Roxboro, Knox, and Mangum Streets for about 1 mile. Saltbox Seafood Joint will be on the left.

AFTER EATING If it has been a while since you have been in Durham, drive down Magnum St. to the center of town and marvel at the transformation of the downtown.

Bob's Bar-B-Q

1589 Lake Road, Creedmoor, NC 27522 · (919) 528-2081
Monday–Saturday 10:00 A.M.–8:00 P.M.; closed Sunday

At Bob's, you order at the counter and then sit down at one of the friendly long tables. The late Harry Coleman, editor of the local newspaper, once explained to me that the barbecue at Bob's doesn't fit neatly into either the Lexington or the Eastern North Carolina style. "It's just good, mild barbecue." The vinegar-based sauce is the late Bob Whitt's recipe that customers enjoyed when he ran his original restaurant in Roxboro.

But there's no question about it being North Carolina barbecue. The pork shoulders are cooked long and slow, and they have just the right flavor, especially for someone who is just about to drive into Virginia from North Carolina and wants to taste our barbecue for the last time. Owners Paula Ellington and Carla Magnum are the twin granddaughters of Bob Whitt, the original Bob. They're continuing the family tradition, making sure that everything is clean and bright, that visitors are greeted, and that the barbecue has the same fresh taste that made their family famous for more than a half-century.

And don't leave without tasting the chocolate chess pie or the pecan pie, made fresh daily.

FROM I-85 Take Exit 191 (NC 56/Butner/Creedmoor). Go east toward Creedmoor. Go about 0.5 mile. Bob's is on the left.

AFTER EATING Drive into downtown Creedmoor and inspect the First National Bank Building at 302 Main St. It was built in 1912 and is on the National Register of Historic Places. It is a 2-story, Beaux-Arts-style building. Raised bands of brick cross the first-floor front elevation and explode in sunbursts over 3 round-arched openings.

*Bob's Bar-B-Q
in Creedmoor*

BBQ Barn

*102 West B Street, Butner, NC 27509 · (919) 575-6068
Monday–Saturday 5:30 A.M.–8:00 P.M.; closed Sunday
www.ncagr.gov/ncproducts/ShowSite.asp?ID=100843*

Owner Roger Cooke explains, "We are just a simple, small-town restaurant with great food and a great staff. You will feel right at home here."

The surroundings are modest. The food and fellowship are

the draw. In addition to the barbecue, there are daily "blue plate" specials, which include two vegetables, bread, and a beverage, along with an entrée like stew beef, barbecued chicken, meat loaf, chicken and dumplings, or hamburger steak.

FROM I-85 Take Exit 189, and go 1 mile east on Gate 2 Rd. (which becomes Central Ave.) toward Butner. Turn left on B St. (the second left after the railroad tracks). BBQ Barn is the first building on the right.

....

Skipper Forsyth's Bar-B-Q

2362 N. Garnett Street, Henderson, NC 27537 · (252) 438-5228
Monday–Thursday 10:00 A.M.–8:00 P.M.;
Friday–Saturday 10:00 A.M.–9:00 P.M.; closed Sunday
Summer: Monday–Saturday 10:00 A.M.–9:00 P.M.

Skipper Forsyth opened his restaurant in 1946, and he still watches over it. Well, his portrait takes up a prominent place overlooking the current owner, Regina Ellis, Skipper's granddaughter, as she runs the restaurant. Skipper's remains popular with locals, especially at lunchtime, according to Dorothy Pierce. "Especially at lunch," she told me, "we get big crowds."

Barbecue is a big draw, but the combination plate that adds Brunswick stew and fried chicken with vegetables could make for a great good-bye feast for a traveler headed north.

I almost ordered the less expensive child's plate when I saw that it included "10 and under only or 65 and older."

One of U.S. Representative George Holding's friends told me that he gets a call whenever the congressman is coming to Henderson, saying, "Let's eat at Skipper Forsyth's."

FROM I-85 Take Exit 217 toward Henderson onto Satterwhite Point Rd. (NC 1319). Go 1 mile and turn right onto US 158 East (North Garrett St.). Go 0.2 mile. Skipper Forsyth's will be on the left.

AFTER EATING Visit the site of Henderson High School (now Henderson Middle School), where television personality Charlie Rose was a star basketball player. It is in downtown Henderson at 219 Charles St.

. . . .

Nunnery-Freeman Barbecue

1816 Norlina Road, Henderson, NC 27536 · (252) 438-4751
Tuesday–Saturday 10:00 A.M.–8:30 P.M.;
Sunday 10:00 A.M.–8:00 P.M.

Nunnery-Freeman Barbecue may be one of your last chances to get traditional North Carolina barbecue if you're driving into Virginia.

Some people would say it is your best chance as well.

When the *Charlotte Observer*'s Jack Betts wrote an article about his 10 favorite barbecue places in North Carolina several years ago, Nunnery-Freeman was at the top of the list. Betts says, "We've driven the 45 miles from Raleigh just to pick up a couple of their tender, succulent barbecue sandwiches, but when we have time and rip-roaring appetites, we get the full spread of chopped barbecue, slaw, hushpuppies and the best Brunswick stew in the Piedmont. Banana pudding's the dessert special on Thursdays."

This restaurant has a big fan base in North Carolina even though it does not cook its barbecue in a pit. In fact, Nunnery-Freeman is the reason a lot of North Carolina barbecue restaurants no longer cook over wood. The Nunnery-Freeman folks invented an electric cooker that is sold all over the world.

Gary Freeman, son of the inventor and the current owner, had his own popular restaurant, Gary's Barbecue, for many years. He has merged Gary's with Nunnery-Freeman at the current location.

FROM I-85 Take Exit 217 toward Henderson onto Satterwhite Point Rd. (NC 1319). Go 1 mile and turn right onto US 158 East (North Garrett St.). Go 1 mile. Nunnery-Freeman will be on the left, next door to Two Twenty Seafood Restaurant. (Note: Be careful in searching for the restaurant. You could get directions to the nearby Nunnery-Freeman Manufacturing Co.)

....

Whistle Stop Cafe

123 Hyco Street, Norlina, NC 27563 · (252) 456-0855
Monday–Friday 11:00 A.M.–8:00 P.M.; closed Saturday–Sunday
NO CREDIT CARDS

Norlina is a couple of miles off I-85, just south of the Virginia line. Hence its name and slogan from the town's website: "Norlina, where North Carolina begins." So it's the last place to get North Carolina–style home cooking for northbound travelers and the first place to touch down on the way back home.

I asked for help in finding a good local eatery from Jennifer Harris, editor of the *Warren Record* in nearby Warrenton. She wrote, "There's a restaurant in Norlina called Whistle Stop Cafe that has been around awhile. Home cooking for lunch and dinner, closed on Sundays, locally owned and operated. They have daily specials (Thursday is chicken livers!), and my personal favorite menu item (which I get every time I go) is the country-fried steak with gravy and onions on my mashed taters, another side and sweet tea, of course! They have some homemade desserts that change daily."

This was great news. Just the kind of place I look for. I learned later that Jennifer's paper had awarded the Whistle Stop top honors for Warren County restaurants.

When I visited the Whistle Stop Cafe, Sheila Arnold, one of a team of cheerful, friendly women who work there, greeted me. Sheila brought me the Tuesday special: fried chicken. I got dark meat, which cost a little bit less than the $7.25 for white meat. Tea is $1.59. The special came with two vegetables.

When I bit into the crispy, juicy chicken, I knew I had come to the right place.

Sheila explained that the owner, Lisa Willis, was too busy in the kitchen to talk. But when Lisa's husband, Ebin, dropped by for lunch, he explained that she liked to stay in the kitchen, leaving the customer service aspects of the business to her carefully selected staff. A good meal, nice people, and a trip back in time.

But don't come without cash. They don't take credit cards. And note that Whistle Stop is closed on weekends.

FROM I-85 *If headed north:* Take Exit 226 and follow Ridgeway-Drewry Rd. toward Ridgeway for about 2.5 miles. Turn left on US 1-158 and go about 2 miles into Norlina. Turn right onto Hyco St. Whistle Stop is on the right.

If headed south: Take Exit 233 and follow US 1 for about 7 miles into Norlina. Turn left onto Hyco St. Whistle Stop is on the right.

AFTER EATING Is there anything else to do in Norlina? Sheila explained that the mayor could open up the railroad museum for me, but I found another gem a few doors away. The hardware store, owned and operated by Judy Hayes, gave me a great chance to experience the flavor of an old-time general store.

First, Hayes showed me bins and bins of all kinds of seeds. Then she demonstrated the micro scales she uses to weigh small amounts of seeds. "I will sell you a package for a couple of dollars, but if you just want 35 cents' worth, I can measure that out for you."

Or, if you have a few extra minutes, you can visit the antique shop in the 1863 depot in the tiny community of Warren Plains, just 2 miles away. From Norlina, follow Warren Plains Rd., King Rd., to Crook's Chapel Rd. Call ahead to check: (252) 432-5445. When TV personality Charlie Rose was a child, his father ran a store near the depot. Rose credits his experience working in the store when he was eight years old for his interest in listening to other people. He told the *Savannah Morning News*, "I was a young kid and I wanted to have conversations with adults; you have to speak to their world. . . . You have to know who they are, what they're about, what their curiosity is, what their experience is, what they're good at. People like to talk. And people like to talk about themselves."

INTERSTATE **95**

I must have traveled along I-95 a hundred times. At every intersection, it seems, there is the same combination of gas stations,
motels, and fast food places. But let me tell you a secret: You can
pull off the interstate almost anywhere between Lumberton and
Roanoke Rapids, drive a few miles in any direction, and run into
a local, family-owned restaurant. Its staff will be friendly and the
locals glad to see you.

But since you might not have time to do the exploring, I have
gathered a group of possible stopping places that will give you the
chance to dine at restaurants owned by members of the Lumbee
tribe, at several popular all-you-can-eat buffets, and at some highly
praised Eastern-style barbecue restaurants.

If you like to eat a lot, you will love the way country cooking
is usually served at some of the places along I-95. It is often buf-
fet-style and sometimes "all you can eat."

In fact, after you visit some of the places I am going to describe,
I bet you will start calling I-95 "the Boulevard of Buffets."

Driving north on I-95 you will also run into some of North
Carolina's best-known barbecue restaurants. I am not going to start
taking sides about what kind of North Carolina barbecue—Eastern
or Lexington—is better. But if you like the Eastern style, then driving up I-95 as you approach the Virginia line could be your pathway
to paradise.

Unfortunately, most of us are afraid to take the extra few
minutes to explore, instead rushing to some important meeting or

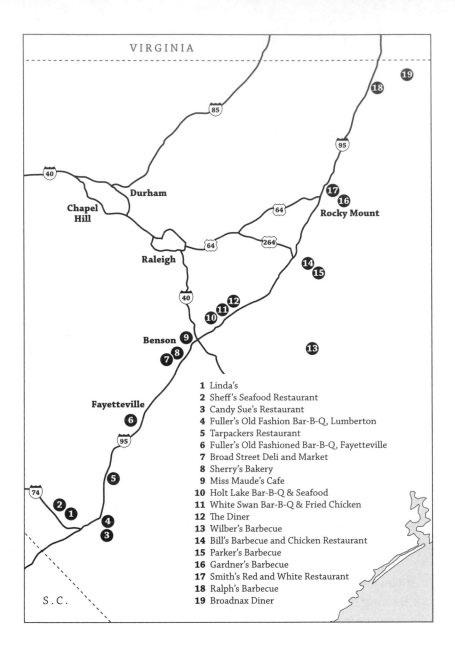

1 Linda's
2 Sheff's Seafood Restaurant
3 Candy Sue's Restaurant
4 Fuller's Old Fashion Bar-B-Q, Lumberton
5 Tarpackers Restaurant
6 Fuller's Old Fashioned Bar-B-Q, Fayetteville
7 Broad Street Deli and Market
8 Sherry's Bakery
9 Miss Maude's Cafe
10 Holt Lake Bar-B-Q & Seafood
11 White Swan Bar-B-Q & Fried Chicken
12 The Diner
13 Wilber's Barbecue
14 Bill's Barbecue and Chicken Restaurant
15 Parker's Barbecue
16 Gardner's Barbecue
17 Smith's Red and White Restaurant
18 Ralph's Barbecue
19 Broadnax Diner

hurrying home. And when we get hungry on I-95, we usually breeze through the drive-thru, don't we? Then, later on, we kick ourselves for not being more adventurous.

But here's where I can help. I've found some places for you to visit. It will take you a few extra minutes, but I'm going to try to persuade you that the little bit of extra time will pay off with good food and good memories.

....

Linda's

408 East Third Street, Pembroke, NC 28372 · (910) 521-8127
Monday–Saturday 6:30 A.M.–9:00 P.M.; closed Sunday

Linda's is not only a great place to get a good home-cooked meal. It also gives a visitor a chance to pay a quick visit to the center of life for the Lumbees, the largest group of American Indians in the eastern United States.

When I worked at UNC-Pembroke a few years ago, I always liked to go to Linda's at lunchtime to catch up on local news. Linda Sheppard serves country cooking in a buffet line, and there will always be a short wait. Everybody seems to know everybody else.

The other guests at Linda's won't interrupt your meal, but many will be glad to answer questions about Pembroke or local Indian life. If you make the effort, you might find out some things about Pembroke and the Lumbees that few others know.

FROM I-95 Take Exit 17. Go west on NC 711 for about 10 miles. Linda's is on the left as you come into downtown Pembroke.

AFTER EATING Drive a few blocks to the UNC-Pembroke campus and take a walk, starting at the historic Old Main Building. Inside on the first floor is the Museum of the Southeast American Indian (8:00 A.M.–5:00 P.M., Monday through Saturday, but closed during the noon hour), with displays about Lumbee hero Henry Berry Lowrie, a Robin Hood type, who became an outlaw to avenge the deaths of his father and brother during Civil War times. Also featured is the Lumbee breakup of a Ku Klux Klan rally in 1958.

. . . .

Sheff's Seafood Restaurant

100 East Third Street, Pembroke, NC 28372 · (910) 521-4667
Tuesday–Friday 11:00 A.M.–2:30 P.M. and 5:00 P.M.–9:30 P.M.;
Saturday 4:00 P.M.–9:30 P.M.; closed Sunday

Former UNC-Pembroke chancellor Joe Oxendine introduced me to the treat of eating seafood for supper at Sheff's, especially on Tuesdays, when Sheff (the nickname of James Sheffield) serves spots, a kind of fish, "all you can eat." People come from all over. Dr. Oxendine explained that in the old days spots were cheap fish and all that struggling Lumbees could afford. Now that they can afford to go out to eat and order something more expensive, they still order spots, even though they're not as cheap as they used to be.

FROM I-95 Take Exit 17. Go west on NC 711 for about 11 miles into Pembroke. You will see Sheff's right after you cross the railroad tracks.

AFTER EATING Before or after eating, I like to sit in one of the rocking chairs on Sheff's front porch and wait for the trains to come by. But the town of Pembroke and the university campus also await your exploration.

Candy Sue's Restaurant

111 West Third Street, Lumberton, NC 28358 · (910) 739-8430
Monday–Friday lunch 11:00 A.M.–2:00 P.M.;
Tuesday–Saturday supper 5:00 P.M. "until";
Sunday lunch 11:00 A.M.–3:00 P.M.
candysues.com

In her wonderful book *Literary Trails of Eastern North Carolina*, Georgann Eubanks shares that world-famous author (and Lumberton native) Jill McCorkle has a soft spot for Candy Sue's café. When I checked with McCorkle, she confirmed, saying, "Candy-Sue's is really good home-style food. The chicken salad is wonderful. I love the vegetables and always go straight for the greens and field peas or okra. I think you should definitely include them and eat there!"

Candy Sue's promises that they serve "home-style, southern-style cooking, prepared fresh every day." It all got started in 1998 when Susan Walker—who went to high school with McCorkle—and Candy Borbet, armed with only their recipes, opened a restaurant in a cinderblock building.

In 2012, they moved the booming business to Candy Sue's current location, the former home of Black Water Grill. Since 2005, Susan has been the sole owner of Candy Sue's and, with the help of her son Kevin, continues the tradition of home-style cooking worth writing about.

FROM I-95 Take Exit 19 onto West Carthage Rd. toward downtown Lumberton. Go 1 mile and then continue onto North Water St. and go 0.5 mile. Turn left onto West Third St. Candy Sue's will be on the right.

AFTER EATING Around the corner at 111 West Third St. is the Robeson County History Museum, open on Tuesday and Thursday mornings and Sunday afternoon.

Less than a block away along Water St. you'll find the Lumber River. The old Lumberton Town Commons Park is accessible there, and it is marked by a small monument that, quoting poet John Charles McNeill, lets visitors know that the spot is "a high bluff of the Lumber River, where that stream, describing a gentle curve and overhung by cypress, gum and maple, shows at its best."

For more of the river, Riverwalk is accessible from West Fifth St. It runs along the river from downtown to Luther Britt Park, a walk of approximately 1.5 miles from beginning to end, or a 3-mile roundtrip. It includes areas that overlook the river and is wonderful for bird watching.

....

Fuller's Old Fashion Bar-B-Q, Lumberton

3201 Roberts Avenue, Lumberton, NC 28360 · (910) 738-8694
Monday–Friday 11:00 A.M.–9:00 P.M.;
Saturday 11:30 A.M.–9:00 P.M.; Sunday 11:00 A.M.–4:00 P.M.

In the 1980s, Fuller Locklear, a Lumbee Indian, and his wife, Delora, opened a small restaurant near their home, serving fried chicken and seafood, southern vegetables, and barbecue. From humble beginnings, Fuller's has become a bustling and famous place to eat. With a new addition, the restaurant now seats more than 300 people.

Locklear built a reputation for his collards, which he grew himself. But he would not serve them unless they were fresh and in season. So if you want to eat collards, come in the fall or winter.

Eric Locklear, Fuller and Delora's son, and other family members have continued their parents' work. "My mom always said, 'If you're going to cook, cook with your heart,'" Eric told the *Fayetteville Observer*. "Treat people like family, and feed them like family."

Thomas Ross, emeritus geography professor at UNC-Pembroke, and Scott Bigelow, the university's public relations officer, told me about Fuller's, praising the delicious southern cooking and the variety on their buffet line. When my family and I stopped there

Fuller's Old Fashion Bar-B-Q in Lumberton

early one Sunday afternoon, the restaurant was full with the after-church crowd.

You can order from Fuller's menu if you are not too hungry, but the buffet is hard to resist. It has every kind of vegetable, lots of choices of meats, a giant salad bar, and cobbler, pies, and soft ice cream. All for a modest price.

My friend and former congressional staffer Don DeArmon lives in Maryland. But when his family is on the road to the coast, they like to stop at Fuller's. "They always have a fresh something, this time collards, and we like their deviled crab—even as I'm filling up on rice and black-eyed peas with a side of fresh corn. We also like the vibe. A very friendly mix of locals and travelers."

DeArmon is not alone. *Southern Living* magazine named Fuller's one of the South's top 5 "Great Interstate Highway Barbecue Joints."

FROM I-95 Take Exit 20 (Lumberton/Red Springs). From the intersection, head west on NC 211 toward Red Springs. Go about 0.5 mile. Fuller's is on the left just beyond a Texaco station.

AFTER EATING If you are a fan of Jill McCorkle, drive into Lumberton to visit her hometown and the inspiration for her mythical town of Fulton. The cemetery in her novel *Life after Life* is modeled on Meadow Cemetery, which you can reach by following North Roberts St. into town for about 1 mile and then turning right onto North Walnut St.

. . . .

Tarpackers Restaurant

201 West Broad Street, Saint Pauls, NC 28384 · (910) 865-1560
Tuesday–Wednesday 11:00 A.M.–2:00 P.M.;
Thursday–Friday 11:00 A.M.–9:00 P.M.;
Saturday 5:00 P.M.–9:00 P.M.;
Sunday 11:00 A.M.–2:00 P.M.; closed Monday
www.tarpackers.com

The name "Tarpackers" comes, of course, from a combination of "Tar Heel" and "Wolfpack," two nicknames of our state's rival public universities. Tarpackers doesn't try to settle the argument about which school is better.

In October 2011, Phyllis Williams acquired Tarpackers from former owners Linwood and Sara Hayes. Williams continues to celebrate the history and tradition of both schools. The food is simple, light, and reasonably priced. She says, "The ribs we serve on Thursday, Friday, and Saturday evenings continue be a favorite."

FROM I-95 Take Exit 31 (NC 29/Saint Pauls). Head east on NC 20 (Broad St.) and go 1 mile.

AFTER EATING Take a minute to visit the famous Joe Sugar's clothing store just a few doors away.

Fuller's Old Fashioned Bar-B-Q, Fayetteville

113 North Eastern Boulevard, Fayetteville, NC 28301
(910) 484-5109
Monday–Saturday 11:00 A.M.–9:00 P.M.;
Sunday 11:00 A.M.–6:00 P.M.
www.Fullersbbq.com

If you missed Fuller's in Lumberton or can't wait until you get there to eat, you are in luck. Fuller Locklear's children have opened a branch of Fuller's in Fayetteville with a buffet just like the original. It serves the same barbecue as the original Lumberton restaurant. It is all cooked on the grounds of the Locklear homeplace, where Fuller began more than 20 years ago.

FROM I-95 Take Exit 52. Follow NC 24 west toward Fayetteville for 3 miles. Turn left onto North Eastern Blvd. (I-95 Business/US 301) for 0.3 mile.

AFTER EATING Only about 2 miles from Fuller's, via Grove St. and Rowan St., is the world-class Airborne & Special Operations Museum, which honors and preserves the legendary feats of the airborne and special operations troops. Wonderful, gripping exhibits. Free admission.

Other nearby eateries Stephenson's Bar-B-Q and Meadow Village Restaurant are described in the I-40 chapter.

Broad Street Deli and Market

129 East Broad Street, Dunn, NC 28334 · (910) 891-1002
Monday–Saturday 11:00 A.M.–3:00 P.M.; closed Sunday
broadstreetdeliandmarket.com

Broad Street Deli is not a typical meat-and-three diner, but it has become one of the favorite lunch spots in Dunn. Owners Jamie and Jeff Adkins take pride in their salads, soups, and sandwiches. Carroll Leggett, who grew up in Harnett County and is well known for his knowledge of North Carolina history, politics, and food, says, "Really an oasis. Upbeat with small wine shop, culinary treats to take on the road. Jamie Adkins, the owner, radiates warmth and the spot is a welcoming environment. Excellent chicken gumbo soup—one of my favorites—and hot ham and cheese on good bread."

Southern Living recently raved about Broad Street's pimento cheese. Co-owner Jamie plugs the signature sandwich called "The Life of Riley" and full of roast beef and brie with plum sauce or mustard. It is named after Jamie and Jeff's son, Riley.

Every year Broad Street hosts a reunion for the Dunn High School classes of 1961–64. Retired pharmacist Cliff Butler returns each year. He has a special connection to the deli's location. The building was the site of his father's drugstore, Butler and Carroll. Cliff says, "It still has the original floors that I mopped thousands of times as a teenager, and the soda fountain that was built into the store in 1927 is still there."

FROM I-95 Take Exit 73 for US 421/NC 55 toward Dunn/Clinton. Turn right onto East Broad St. and go 1 mile. Broad Street Deli will be on the right.

AFTER EATING Next door at Wisteria is a shop full of "antiques, collectibles, vintage, gifts, and more." At 109 North Wilson is LadyBugsInTheAttic for another selection of antiques and prim-itives. Walk along Broad and Wilson Streets to get a feeling for a small-town downtown, and visit Sherry's Bakery (see below), where you can sample fresh pastries and cakes or just enjoy the aroma of baking bread.

. . . .

Sherry's Bakery

122 North Wilson Street, Dunn, NC 28334
Monday–Saturday 6:00 A.M.–6:00 P.M.; closed Sunday
www.facebook.com/SherrysBakery

Sherry's is another non-meat-and-three that has become a local hotspot. Dunn natives Cliff and Linda Butler recommend Sherry's. Cliff writes, "My standard order is two (sometimes three) hot dogs all the way with an order of fried okra. I never leave without a box full of the pastries. My favorite is the chocolate covered sugar coated honey bun, which I drizzle with half & half and coat with a little butter before microwaving. This is a must try and well worth any fat or diabetes it may cause.

"Linda's dad was a member of the Wisdom Table, which meets every morning at Sherry's. It only takes one vote to become a member and you can vote for yourself. No subject is off limits and every world problem is solved by this group."

Owner Freddie Williford gave me a Wisdom Table membership card with the Rules & Benefits on the reverse side, requiring me "to be truthful most of the time." The bakery opened in 1945. Freddie and his wife, Mary, bought it in 1967 and named it after their six-year-old daughter. Today Sherry Williford Baysa and her brother, Fred, help manage Sherry's. Sadly, Mary died a few years ago. Freddie, born in 1932, is planning his retirement. "When I get to be 100 years old, I am going to hang it up—in 2032." In the meantime, every day Fred and his crew at Sherry's will be making and selling 75–100 dozen donuts, 55 pounds of chicken salad, and numerous pies, cakes, and other pastries.

FROM I-95 Take Exit 73 for US 421/NC 55 toward Dunn/Clinton. Turn right onto East Broad St. and go 1 mile to North Wilson Ave. Sherry's is on the right at the corner.

AFTER EATING Just a few blocks away at 209 West Devine St. is the Gen. William C. Lee House. It contains offices for the Dunn Area Chamber of Commerce and a museum memorial to the Dunn native who was a pioneer of U.S. airborne troops, first commander of the army's jump school at Fort Benning, commander of the then newly formed 101st Airborne Division, and a major planner for the D-Day airborne operations.

. . . .

Miss Maude's Cafe

206 East Main Street, Benson, NC 27504 · (919) 207-9000
Sunday 7:00 A.M.–2:00 P.M.; Monday–Tuesday 6:00 A.M.–2:00 P.M.;
Wednesday–Saturday 6:00 A.M.–8:00 P.M.
www.facebook.com/MissMaudeCafe

Miss Maude's took over the site of the Benson Main Street Café. New owner Cora Godwin's middle name is Maude, but she named the restaurant after her grandmother. Although she has spiffed the place up, she's kept the original counter and booths, as well as the old-time southern cooking and special plates of meat and vegetables.

Mary Davis has been working at Miss Maude's for about 4 years. Smiling brightly, she told me, "We have a good time and cut up with our customers. They are part of our family."

I asked her what brought her to Benson. Then I looked down and saw a bunch of rings on her ring finger and said that it must have been because of a man. "Oh, no," she said, "those are just to keep men from hitting on me. Still, sometimes they give me pieces of paper with their phone numbers. I put them in a jar at home and I've got a jar full."

Mary gave me a sample of Miss Maude's signature dish, chicken salad. When my wife, Harriet, tasted it, she said it was wonderful and bought a pint, which was worth the trip to Benson.

FROM I-95 Take Exit 79 and follow East Main St. toward downtown Benson for 0.5 mile. Miss Maude's is on the left.

AFTER EATING Within a block of Miss Maude's is an old-time pharmacy, a hardware store, an antique-thrift store, and Jenny's Sweet Creations at 221 E. Main St. Jenny's specializes in cakes, but "We always have a candy case full of fresh made candy." Take a walk around the town and visit shops like Tiny, the Modeler's Hobby Shop at 102 N. Market St. For me Benson is like a trip back to the 1950s.

....

Holt Lake Bar-B-Q & Seafood

3506 US 301 South, Smithfield, NC 27577 · (919) 934-0148
Monday 11:00 A.M.–2:00 P.M.;
Tuesday–Saturday 11:00 A.M.–9:00 P.M.; closed Sunday

Brothers Kevin and Terry Barefoot and their wives, Donna and Lori, serve wonderful family-style meals almost all day long at Holt Lake Bar-B-Q & Seafood. You can order from the menu, but if you have my kind of appetite, you will want to eat family-style, which is available if you have at least four people in your group. Believe me, it is worth a special trip for the barbecue and fried chicken, and for a little bit more, you can add shrimp and fish to your choices.

The Barefoots own hundreds of acres of nearby farmland where they raise the hogs for barbecuing and some of the other foods served at Holt Lake.

What struck me about the Barefoots is their devotion to their customers and community. In 2010, a fire swept through the restaurant, and many where unsure if Holt Lake would ever reopen. But the Barefoots had faced this challenge before and persevered—in 1981, a fire had demolished the restaurant, but they banded together and were serving quality 'cue in 60 days. That is dedication.

Kevin and Terry made their mother, a retired teacher's assistant at nearby Four Oaks Elementary School, a partner in the business from the beginning. Although she died in early 2014, her welcoming spirit is still felt at Holt Lake.

FROM I-95 Take Exit 90. Head north on US 301. Go 1.5 miles.

AFTER EATING The restaurant's name comes from Holt's Lake, a private lake for adjoining property owners. You can get a quick look at the lake, the homes, and a golf course by driving along Country Club Rd., which begins 0.1 mile south of the restaurant.

···

White Swan Bar-B-Q & Fried Chicken

3198 US 301 South, Smithfield, NC 27577 · (919) 934-8913
Monday–Wednesday 10:30 A.M.–7:30 P.M.;
Thursday–Saturday 10:30 A.M.–8:30 P.M.;
Sunday 10:30 A.M.–5:00 P.M.

The White Swan in Smithfield is an old-time barbecue place, just like the roadhouses of days gone by. Lynwood Parker owns and runs the White Swan, along with the adjoining motel and an accounting business, and is very active in the political life of Johnston County.

Parker's family has long owned White Swan, but before the Parkers took over, there was a different kind of business on the hill. Known as Flowers' Tavern, it was built in 1930 by Percy Flowers, who grew up in nearby Archers Lodge. Flowers was a legendary moonshiner who made much more money making and selling whisky than he did at the tavern. In his book *Lost Flowers*, Perry Sullivan, Flowers's son, writes that by the 1950s Flowers "was a high-rolling whiskey millionaire." By then Flowers had long since sold the restaurant.

Later it was acquired by Lynwood Parker and his parents. He says that it's a classic southern family business, with all generations of the Parker clan pitching in. "We've had four generations interested in the business," he says, "and we're proud of it. The essence of life in the South is small family farms and businesses. So we're proud to be a part of that heritage."

Bob Garner brags about White Swan's barbecue in *North Carolina Barbecue: Flavored by Time*. Barbecue is the specialty, but there is great fried chicken, Brunswick stew, and ribs.

The restaurant is cozy, with a lot of its business done at the counter, with folks streaming in to get an order to take out. When I sat down and placed my order of barbecue and slaw, my meal was delivered to the table in less than a minute, along with a helping of some of the best hushpuppies I ever ate.

FROM I-95 Take Exit 90. Head north on US 301. Go 2 miles (passing Holt Lake). White Swan is on the left.

AFTER EATING Ask Lynwood Parker to talk to you about Percy Flowers or modern-day North Carolina politics.

. . . .

The Diner

314 East Market Street, Smithfield, NC 27577 · (919) 934-6644
Monday–Friday 6:30 A.M.–2:00 P.M.;
Saturday 6:30 A.M.–11:00 A.M.; closed Sunday

Every small county seat town needs a small diner near its courthouse, a place where the lawyers and court officials can meet. For many years Shirley's, a classic downtown-style diner, served Smithfield's locals until it closed, leaving a void. About 10 years ago, Miami natives Larry and Amy Holt moved to North Carolina and came to the rescue by opening The Diner. It fills the bill for locals

The Diner in Smithfield

and gives visitors the chance to share a piece of small-town life at breakfast and lunch.

Larry and Amy have specials every weekday. Meat and two vegetables for $6.95. The most popular days, they say, are Monday for Larry's special meat loaf and Friday for fried flounder.

FROM I-95 Take Exit 95 to East Market St. Go 1 mile. The Diner will be on the left.

AFTER EATING Visit the celebrated Ava Gardner Museum across the street. Walk down a few blocks to the Smithfield Neuse River Walk's entrance on South Front St. Take a look at the courthouse. Stop in the library, the visitors' center, and the local heritage center for information and displays of local history, all within walking distance.

Wilber's Barbecue

4172 US 70 East, Goldsboro, NC 27534 · (919) 778-5218
Open every day, 6:00 A.M.–9:00 P.M.

Maybe you think Wilber's Barbecue doesn't belong in this book—
no matter how good it is—because it's too far from the interstate.
Goldsboro is almost 30 miles from I-95. You will have to budget an
extra 30-plus minutes to get there and the same amount of time to
get back. So why am I including Wilber's? Here's the reason: I would
go a long way out of my way to eat with Wilber Shirley. The food is
great—especially the barbecue and fried chicken. The experience
of eating at Wilber's should not be denied to any North Carolinian.
In *North Carolina Barbecue: Flavored by Time*, Bob Garner says that
Wilber's is one of only a handful of restaurants in eastern North
Carolina "where barbecue is cooked entirely over hardwood coals."

If you ask former journalist and barbecue expert Jack Betts
about North Carolina's best, here is what he says: "If the question is
best barbecue, period, then my answer is Wilber Shirley's peppery,
chopped barbecue cooked the old way—over hardwood coals just
behind his one-story, redbrick restaurant on Goldsboro's east side."

FROM I-95 *If headed north:* Take Exit 95 (Goldsboro). Head east on
US 70 Business. Follow US 70 Bypass. Wilber's is about 4 miles east
of Goldsboro.

If headed south: Take Exit 119 to I-795 South (US 117-264). Follow I-795 to Goldsboro. At Exit 24 take US 70 Bypass East. Wilber's
is about 4 miles east of Goldsboro.

Bill's Barbecue and Chicken Restaurant

3007 Downing Street, Wilson, NC 27893 · (252) 237-4372
Tuesday–Saturday 11:00 A.M.–8:30 P.M.;
Sunday 11:00 A.M.–8:00 P.M.; closed Monday
www.bills-bbq.com

Bill's is a part of a Bill Ellis mega-complex that takes up a city block. A catering business, a separate take-out building, and a meeting center surround the restaurant.

During a recent North Carolina Writers' Conference at Barton College in Wilson, I slipped away to Bill Ellis's for a plateful of barbecue. When I got there, I noticed that everyone else was lining up at the long buffet. I checked it out and found that not only could I get my barbecue with fixings, but I could get a plate full of country vegetables, fried chicken, and other meats. Afterward, I went back to the line to sample the desserts. They were wonderful, but a sample was all that I could handle. I was just too full to finish. The tab was about $10.

Next time, I am going to fast for a day or two before I go back to Bill's, just to be sure that I have room for the pudding and cobbler.

Part of the fun at Bill's is the long tables where you might find yourself seated by somebody you have never seen before. You will start out as strangers, but before it is over, you might have a new best friend. And if you don't like your company, you will find hundreds of other possible seats in this gigantic facility.

FROM I-95 Take Exit 119A-119B to I-795 South (US 117-264) and follow I-795 South for 4 miles. Take Exit 42 and follow Downing St. for 1.5 miles. Bill's will be on the right.

AFTER EATING Take a quick trip (about 2 miles) to downtown Wilson via Downing St. and Goldsboro St. and visit the site of the planned Vollis Simpson Whirlijig Park at 301 Goldsboro St. It features Simpson's whimsical moving machines that drew thousands of visitors to his farm. According to the park's website, it anchors an effort to draw visitors to Wilson, where "weathered brick tobacco warehouses, 'five & dime' stores and a Classical Revival courthouse share newly renovated street space and signage with today's boutique shoppes, regional business incubator and burgeoning arts community."

....

Parker's Barbecue, Wilson

2514–2580 US 301, Wilson, NC 27893 · (252) 237-0972
Open every day, 9:00 A.M.–8:45 P.M.

First of all, let's set the record straight. There is some discussion about Parker's—maybe even some controversy. It is mostly about two questions. The first is whether Parker's is too far away from I-95, and too confusing to find, to be considered close and convenient enough to interrupt a long-distance trip.

The other question has to do with whether Parker's mostly gas-cooked barbecue can meet the standards of the barbecue purist.

Having raised these questions, about which there will always be debate, I can say with certainty that Parker's is well worth a stop.

Especially if you are hungry. Especially if you want to see a lot of local people enjoying the ceremonies of fellowship and eating large quantities of country-style cooked food.

Even if you have questions about the distance or the gas, don't pass by Parker's at mealtime if you are anywhere close by.

Some barbecue experts simply overlook the gas controversy and make their judgments on the results. For instance, Jack Betts praised Parker's a few years ago, writing about the "authentic, slightly dry Eastern North Carolina barbecue, and corn sticks that remind you that they still do things the good old way at The Original Parker's."

Why does it still taste so good? Eric Lippard, one of the managers of Parker's, reminded me, "It is still pit cooked barbecue, and there aren't enough trees in North Carolina to cook it all."

Some fans, including New York chef and North Carolina barbecue expert Elizabeth Karmel, praise Parker's for other reasons. Karmel wrote in the May 2015 issue of *Saveur* about Parker's fried chicken, "This is the best chicken I've ever had in my life. It was so good that, the first time I had it, I got up and asked the owner of the restaurant how he made it. They do it really simply, very old-fashioned. It's got the crispiest skin, not greasy at all, and the place feels straight out of the 1950s."

It goes back even further, back to 1946, when three brothers started Parker's. In 1986, Don Williams, who had been working at Parker's since 1963, became the owner. In 1996, Eric Lippard and Kevin Lamm joined him as partners and managers. One of them is almost always on-site, and they welcome questions from their customers.

Eric was greeting customers at the door and charmed former Wake County School Board chair Patti Head. She had driven from Raleigh to meet her sister, Cookie Cantwell, who lives in Wilmington. They said they chose Parker's as their meeting place "because it's an institution, and everybody is so friendly, like Eric."

FROM I-95 Take Exit 119A-119B to I-795 South (US 117-264) and follow I-795 South for 5 miles. Take Exit 43A to US 301 North toward Wilson. Go 2 miles. Parker's is on the left.

AFTER EATING Ask Eric Lippard to tell you the secret of Parker's highly praised fried chicken. Make a quick visit to Barton College (formerly Atlantic Christian College) about 4 miles away at 200 East Access Dr.

Gardner's Barbecue

1331 North Wesleyan Boulevard, Rocky Mount, NC 27804
(252) 446-2983
Sunday–Thursday 10:00 A.M.–9:00 P.M.;
Friday–Saturday 10:00 A.M.–9:30 P.M.
www.gardnerfoods.com

Judging from the long line of folks waiting to eat at Gardner's Barbecue the last time I was there, its reputation is still going strong. Inside, most customers were eating all they wanted, choosing either to go through a buffet line or to be served family-style at the table. As good and plentiful as the food is, there is more to Gardner's than just eating.

The lively red-and-white table coverings are just part of the reason it is so bright and cheerful. People there smile at each other—and at strangers. It honestly made me feel I was at a church supper rather than a restaurant.

When the cash register attendants were too busy counting money to talk to me, Gloria Davis, the assistant manager, took me under her wing and answered all my questions. She told me that her boss, Gerry Gardner, brother of former congressman and lieutenant governor Jim Gardner, maintains the long family association with this country restaurant. Since that visit, Gerry's sons, Jay and Jaime, have purchased the company from their father and completed a major remodeling, which they promise will not affect the restaurant's reputation. They say, "We appreciate our loyal customers who have supported us for over 40 years and we plan to continue offering the same great tasting Eastern N.C. style BBQ and down home cooking for years to come."

FROM I-95 Take Exit 138 to merge onto US 64 East toward Rocky Mount. Go 3.8 miles to and take Exit 468A for Wesleyan Blvd./US 301. Turn left on North Wesleyan Blvd. for 1.5 miles. Gardner's will be on the right.

AFTER EATING Visit the campus of North Carolina Wesleyan College, about 3.5 miles north on Wesleyan Blvd.

....

Smith's Red and White Restaurant

3635 North Halifax Road, Rocky Mount, NC 27804 · (252) 443-0418
Tuesday–Saturday 6:30 A.M.–2:00 P.M.; closed Sunday–Monday
www.smithsredandwhite.com

Pat Ashley, who travels all over eastern North Carolina working with our public schools, got my attention with her enthusiasm for this place. She wrote, "Smith's restaurant is a superior southern meat and vegetable breakfast and lunch spot beside Smith's Red and White grocery right off I-95 just north of Rocky Mount. The menu of meats and vegetables changes daily. Always three or four different meats: smothered pork chops, fried chicken, meat loaf, as well as rare items like backbones. They have the best squash and rutabagas I have ever eaten as well as cheese biscuits to die for. There is a small order menu with things like oysters in addition to the meat and vegetables daily specials, which are served cafeteria-style. I always bring home a take-out meal because it is better than anywhere I have found for real, old style but high quality southern food from the 1950's."

Three generations of the Smith family have nurtured the food in Dortches since 1954 when S. B. (Sherwood) Smith began a small grocery business in the corner of a nearby farm supply store. In 1964, he moved to a cinderblock building and expanded the grocery business to include pork processing.

About this time, S. B.'s son, Bruce, joined the business, and in 1999, Bruce's son, Derrick, signed on. The expanded grocery operations have thrived, and in 2010 the Smiths added the restaurant to feed the many visitors and to take advantage of the grocery's supply of fresh vegetables and meats.

Smith's Red and White Grocery in Rocky Mount

FROM I-95 Take Exit 141 and turn onto NC 43 (Dortches Blvd.) toward Rocky Mount. Go 0.3 mile and turn left onto North Halifax Rd. Red and White will be on the right.

AFTER EATING Stop by the grocery next door. It is even better known than the restaurant. People travel from all over, coolers with them, to load up on the great sausage and specialty items, especially during the holiday season, when the store is decked out in holiday cheer. The sausage makes a great present in any season. For sweets to take home, stop by Tastee Creations Bakery and ask Hazel Armstrong about her special sweet potato bread. Across the parking lot are two shops, Huck's Antiques and Exit 141 Collections, both of which have an eclectic set of offerings. Both are owned by local men who just do not want to move away. If you have more time, take a look at the Dortches House, built in Federal style about 1810 and listed on the National Register of Historic Places. It is at 4976 Dortches Blvd., "catty-cornered" across from Red and White but covered with woods and vines. It is not visible from the road and is so hidden that many of the locals do not even know it is there.

. . . .

Ralph's Barbecue

1400 Julian R. Allsbrook Highway, Weldon, NC 27890
(252) 536-2102
Open every day, 9:00 A.M.–8:30 P.M.

You could argue all you want with Wes Woodruff, a Roanoke Rapids native who now lives in Orlando, Florida, but you are not likely to change his firm opinion that Eastern style is the "only kind of barbecue." Nor will you persuade him that Ralph's is not the best place in North Carolina to eat. Woodruff declares, "My wife and I usually get back to Roanoke Rapids twice a year or so, and Ralph's is a mandatory stop. We usually get several pounds of barbecue and several quarts of Brunswick stew, freeze it, and bring it back to Orlando, where we share it with some of our friends from North Carolina."

As much as Woodruff enjoys the barbecue, it is not his favorite dish. "Ralph's Brunswick stew is the best I have ever had, and that includes the stew served in Brunswick, Georgia."

Like Woodruff, I love barbecue and Brunswick stew and also the hushpuppies and banana pudding. But sometimes I like variety and quantity. That is why I timed my visit to Ralph's at suppertime when the buffet line was open. At lunchtime, after 5:00 P.M., and all day Saturday and Sunday, you can sample the country vegetables, fried chicken, barbecue, and other meats. I tested all of Woodruff's favorites, too, and left about $10 poorer with a very full tummy.

Wes Woodruff says that he is not kin to Ralph and Mason Woodruff, who started Ralph's back in 1946. But when you visit, you can check the history with Mason's daughter Kim Amerson, who runs the family restaurant today.

*Ralph's Barbecue
in Weldon*

FROM I-95 Take Exit 173 (Weldon/Roanoke Rapids). Head east on
US 158 (Julian R. Allsbrook Hwy.). Go 2 blocks.

AFTER EATING Visit the Roanoke Canal Trail, which runs from
Water St. in Weldon to the Roanoke Canal Museum at 15 Jackson
St. in Roanoke Rapids.

Broadnax Diner

306 Park Street, Seaboard, NC 27876 · (252) 589-2292
Monday–Friday 6:00 A.M.–2:30 P.M.;
Saturday: 6:00 A.M.–11:00 A.M.; closed Sunday

If you want to experience small-town eastern North Carolina the way it used to be, stop by the Broadnax Diner for a meal, as I did one Saturday morning. Owners Johnnie and Carolyn Lassiter were working hard behind the counter trying to keep up with the hungry crowd of customers. They fixed me a "big breakfast" with eggs, bacon, sausage, hash browns, and salmon cakes while I learned about the prospects for the corn and peanut crops from a local farmer. The Lassiters bought the restaurant some years ago from the family of Seaboard's mayor, Melvin Broadnax. Their only request, according to Carolyn Lassiter, "was that we keep the name, which we have been proud to do."

FROM I-95 Take Exit 176 and follow NC 46 toward Garysburg for 3.5 miles. Turn left onto US 301 and then immediately turn right onto NC 186. Go 7.5 miles and turn right at Park St. in Seaboard.

AFTER EATING Explore the historic former railroad town where famous Broadway designer William Ivey Long was born in 1947 and maintains a second home.

Afterword

Now that you and I are at the end of this book, remember Tolstoy's words about all great literature being either "a stranger comes to town" or "a man goes on a journey." Pretend for a few moments that you visited all these eateries with me. So together we have made ourselves strangers in town at more than a hundred different places, and we are now at the end of a very long journey.

Okay, maybe we have not made great literature, but you and I have book-fulls of stories together.

Before we part, I want to thank you for being my companion and for joining with me in the joy of adventure, surprise, new acquaintances, and a growing appreciation of the rich diversity of the people of our state—and, of course, in so many places some real good home-style cooking.

Let's do it again sometime soon.

Until then,

Thanks!

D. G.

Acknowledgments

Warm thanks to the folks at UNC Press, especially the book's editor, Lucas Church, who made my work better at every turn, and Mark Simpson-Vos, who persuaded me to undertake this venture. My college classmate Bob Auman read every word several times and made great suggestions about new places to consider. Former editors Mary Best and Vicky Jarrett of *Our State* magazine and the others there encouraged me to visit and write about local eateries for their wonderful publications.

This book is the collective effort of countless people who gave me tips about their favorite places, who read selections from the book, who took me to restaurants all over the state, and who encouraged me to continue and complete this project. Some of them are listed here: Shelia Kay Adams, Gene Adcock, Bob Anthony, Chris Arvidson, Bob and Pat Ashley, Bob Auman, Phil Baddour, Alton Balance, Hugh and Brenda Barger, Dr. Ben Barker, Cynthia and Robert Bashford, Bobby Benton, Jack Betts, Mark Bibbs, Scott Bigelow, Catherine Bishir, Charles Blackburn, John Blythe, Al Brand, Gray Brookshire, David Brown, Stephen Bryant, Cliff and Linda Butler, Tom Byers, Cindy Campbell, Donna Campbell, Cookie Cantwell, Pete Chikes, Mike Clayton, Charles Coble, George Couch, Ricky Cox, John Curry, Frank Daniels, Gene Davis, Jan and Jim Dean, Don DeArmon, Henry Doss, Jim Early, Rufus Edmisten, Marion Ellis, Bob Epting, Georgann Eubanks, Marcie Ferris, Stephen Fletcher, Charles and Katherine Frazier, Randy Gardner, Bob Garner, John Goodman, Margie and Tom Haber, Joe Hackney,

Speed Hallman, Jennifer Harris, Patti Head, Tommy Hedrick, Suzanne Hobbs, Charles Holland, Judy Honeycutt Hefner, Elizabeth Hudson, Dick Huffman, Jack and Ruby Hunt, Judy Hunt, Judge Bob Hunter, Hugh Johnston, Betty Kenan, Tom Kenan, Myrtle Kiker, Mal King, John Kuykendall, Betsy Kylstra, Barbara Ledford, William Ivey Long, Bernie Mann, Jamie May, Drake Maynard, Jill McCorkle, Bill McCoy, Stewart McLeod, Grant McRorie, Moreton Neal, Ray Oehler, Nancy Olson, Doug Orr, Joseph Oxendine, Josie Patton, David Perry, Judge Dickson Phillips, Julian Pleasants, Hal Powell, Norfleet Pruden, Allan Pugh, John Railey, John Shelton Reed, Ken Ripley, Wyndham Robertson, John Rogers, Richard Rogers, former judge and UNC president Tom Ross, Professor Tom E. Ross, Sally and David Royster, Marsden Sale, Raleigh Shoemaker, Lee Smith, Moyer Smith, Dick Spangler, John Staples, Shannon Kennedy Stephenson, Shelby Stephenson, Walter Turner, Daniel Wallace, Marcia Webster, Andrea Weigl, Jerry Williams, Bob Woodruff, Thad Woody, and Lynn York.

If I left you off the list, I owe you a meal at one of the eateries in this book.

Acknowledgments

D. G. Martin is host of UNC-TV's *North Carolina Bookwatch*, the state's premier literary series. A graduate of Davidson College and Yale Law School and a former Green Beret, Martin practiced law in Charlotte for 20 years before joining the University of North Carolina, where he served as vice president for public affairs and chief legislative liaison. Since his retirement he has served in interim leadership positions at UNC-Pembroke, North Carolina Central University, Trust for Public Land, Triangle Land Conservancy, and North Carolina's Clean Water Management Trust Fund and as president of the William R. Kenan Jr. Fund. About 40 North Carolina newspapers carry his weekly newspaper column that features books, politics, and related topics.

Other **Southern Gateways Guides** you might enjoy

Lessons from the Sand
Family-Friendly Science Activities You Can Do on a Carolina Beach

CHARLES O. PILKEY AND ORRIN H. PILKEY

Fun ways to learn about the beach and its surrounding environment

Tar Heel History on Foot
Great Walks through 400 Years of North Carolina's Fascinating Past

LYNN SETZER

Day-tripping through our state's vibrant history

Waterfalls and Wildflowers in the Southern Appalachians
Thirty Great Hikes

TIMOTHY P. SPIRA

Includes 125 color photos of wildflowers for plant identification

Available at bookstores, by phone at **1-800-848-6224**, or on the web at **www.uncpress.unc.edu**